AF594837

Postsensual Aesthetics

The MIT Press would like to thank the anonymous peer reviewers who provided comments on drafts of this book. The generous work of academic experts is essential for establishing the authority and quality of our publications. We acknowledge with gratitude the contributions of these otherwise uncredited readers.

This book was set in Univers by The MIT Press. Printed and bound in the United States of America.

Library of Congress Cataloging-in-Publication Data is available.

ISBN: 978-0-262-04760-9

10 9 8 7 6 5 4 3 2 1

Postsensual Aesthetics

ON THE LOGIC OF THE CURATORIAL

James Voorhies

The MIT Press
Cambridge, Massachusetts
London, England

Prelude

Section 1
dOCUMENTA (13)

Interlude

Section 2
DOCUMENTA11

Section 3
CENTRE FOR CONTEMPORARY ART SINGAPORE

Prelude

The Research Exhibition

In 2003, Maria Eichhorn commissioned a historian to conduct provenance research into fifteen works of art in the collection of Munich's Städtische Galerie im Lenbachhaus. The research revealed, or heightened the suspicion, that the paintings had been illicitly confiscated by the Nazis from private and public Jewish collections.[1] Then, in 2015, Eichhorn organized a seminar at the Haus der Kulturen der Welt in Berlin.[2] In collaboration with researchers, the attendees looked into official documents in Berlin's municipal archives disclosing the illegal transfer of Jewish-owned land sold at lower value and under coercion to the state during the Nazi era. The land in question is where the HKW sits today.[3] In 2017, Eichhorn founded the *Rose Valland Institute*, an interdisciplinary project committed to investigating issues related to Nazi-looted property.[4] The launch of the *Institute*, named after the French art historian who kept secret records of plundered art, included a call for papers focusing on orphaned property in Europe and an invitation to citizens to research property believed to be stolen and submit results to the *Institute*. The *Institute* partnered with the Käte Hamburger Center for Advanced Study in the Humanities "Law as Culture" at the University of Bonn and, since 2020, it has operated with support from the Berlin Artistic Research Grant Program.[5] The *Rose Valland Institute* continues to support inquiries into unresolved issues of property ownership relating to the theft of Jewish citizens' possessions in Germany and across Europe.[6]

Maria Eichhorn is an artist. The *Rose Valland Institute* accounted for her participation in *documenta 14* in 2017. In fact, over the course of more than twenty years, Eichhorn has established herself as a formidable voice in work committed to the restoration of dispossessed property and provenance research.[7] Through her work and collaborations with experts, citizens, and institutions, she has invigorated the discourse around these issues, drawing attention to the fact that while 1963 was the deadline set by the Reparations Agreement between Israel and the Federal Republic of Germany to reclaim possessions, many questions still remain unanswered.[8] A large-scale art exhibition like *documenta 14* is an unlikely venue to display the work of an institute dedicated to examining the histories of unlawfully acquired Jewish property. Yet, for all her work as a researcher and facilitator, Maria Eichhorn is nevertheless an artist. She has chosen to undertake this work through contemporary art. But how are visitors to exhibitions expected to understand its complexities and depth? How are curators expected to exhibit and mediate it? How do museums acquire it? How do markets value it? How do critics respond to it? Eichhorn's work cannot be experienced in totality. She has presented a problem to the field of contemporary art.

Eichhorn is not alone. Many artists and curators pursue research with experts like sociologists, anthropologists, political theorists, engineers, and philosophers. The collaborative work might focus on untold histories and overlooked archives, or be niche studies in a field like astronomy, the climate, or urban planning. The work might probe topics related to colonialism, racial inequities, or flows of human migration. The research topic sometimes becomes synonymous with the practice of an artist or a curator. It can be a project they have traced over years—entire careers—and presented in various exhibitions and publications. While they may not have technical training or formal education in the subject, they may often single-handedly recover and draw attention to something, someone, or someplace, hastening a critical discourse about it. Contemporary art is uniquely generous to these types of inquiries. It gives time, attention, space, and resources to this work, with the contemporary exhibition serving as a kind of showcase or clearinghouse.

Postsensual Aesthetics: On the Logic of the Curatorial reflects on these conditions. It offers a rethinking of aesthetic forms in order to provide a theoretical framework for describing and analyzing the production of knowledge by artists and curators as it relates to the contemporary art exhibition. It seeks to problematize and raise questions about what is at stake in the field of art when artistic research mimics the methodologies of traditional research disciplines and aligns itself with them. The following theorization responds to changes over the past three decades in modes of production where artists and curators intentionally and strategically extend aesthetic engagement in contemporary art, from the sensual to the cognitive. It argues for a reconsideration of the centering of the epistemological in contemporary art where complex propositions and projects—like Eichhorn's extraordinary launch of a research institute in *documenta 14*—are deployed using the mechanisms of exhibition. These propositions frequently manifest in the concerted coordination of exhibition and publication, suggesting that audiences are willing and able to reconcile a combination of both sensual and cognitive experiences with the work in order to access, engage, and transform the content offered into knowledge.

Publications (not to be confused with exhibition catalogs) have become essential to this work. They offer a new kind of curatorial challenge—a beautiful problem, if you will—for developing and honing other kinds of curatorial skills and methodologies for mediating content and bringing it to the public. Today, many artists and curators strategically coordinate the real and conceptual qualities of the exhibition and book forms to complement each other. They look to the book as a valuable consolidator for this work because the book does something a physical exhibition cannot: it provides extended time with art and ideas, time that is elastic, time that is on the reader's own terms, allowing information to become knowledge at whatever pace is individually desirable. Books hold the sustained intellectual arguments posited by artists, curators, and their collaborators, expanding and extending work further and longer into the public realm. Books can act as repositories, giving artists and curators opportunities to take stock by publishing something related to a research project that may be ongoing for years and even decades. Books provide opportunities to understand and engage with multifaceted works, like Eichhorn's, so when audiences experience her exhibition at *documenta 14*, they might already be informed of the complexity of her work. Simply put, it helps to know something about a project before or after an exhibition experience because the work is structurally conceived to connect, in part, to audiences through reading—not only within the limited spatial and temporal parameters of an exhibition but also through books outside of it.

These conditions for producing and disseminating knowledge in contemporary art have transformed the exhibition into a dynamic arena for theoretical thinking and research over the past thirty years. Informed by exhibitions like documenta, Istanbul Biennial, Guangzhou Triennial, Gwangju Biennale, Manifesta, and Bienal de São Paulo, the field of contemporary art has proven to be a discursive space for dialogue among participants entering from a range of disciplines to work alongside artists and curators. Advances in curating and publishing have contributed to the contemporary exhibition's unprecedented expansion and influence on understanding and learning through art. Yet the common way of recognizing aesthetic value remains concerned with the sensual experience of the viewer and the autonomy of the discrete art object.

Traditional aesthetics is indifferent to the multifaceted qualities of the exhibition form that brings content into the public realm through the cognitive experience of reading. Aesthetics grapples with what is interpreted and trafficked as art in relation to what is understood as everyday images and scenes. Jacques Rancière reminds us that aesthetics is grounded in the mitigation between human nature and representation:

> From Kant to Adorno, including Schiller, Hegel, Schopenhauer and Nietzsche, the object of aesthetic discourse has only ever been to think through this discordant relation. What this discourse has thereby striven to articulate is not the fantasy of speculative minds, but the new and paradoxical regime for identifying what is recognizable as art. I have proposed to call this regime the aesthetic regime of art.[9]

To Rancière's point, art is different from everyday life. For more than two centuries, aesthetic criteria have developed with philosophies on the sensual aesthetic experience of art, influenced by Kant and, more recently, theories on the autonomy of the art object by Adorno. Sensual perception is the basis for aesthetic judgment, which refutes the production of recognizable forms of knowledge communicated through language. Ways of knowing, for these philosophers and their adherents, occurs in and through the experience of the senses. Their ideas were advanced by modernist critics such as Clement Greenberg and Michael Fried who, among others, were interested in the aesthetic dimensions of the object as it relates to the visual, aural, and bodily experiences of the spectator. In order for art to exist, a form of thought and framework to identify it needs to exist. This form of thought helps separate art from everyday sensory experiences.

Can we apply theories of aesthetics offered by Kant, Adorno, and Rancière to multifaceted, research-based practices that strategically think through how a constellation of factors—including reading—combine to form the total work? Analyses of visual art tend to look toward theories of aesthetics based on how the body, eyes, and ears interpret the material world—viewers versus artworks. Yet work like Eichhorn's is conceived, produced, and distributed as part of contemporary art exhibitions. It exists. But the aesthetic regime of art, to use Rancière's term, is not equipped to analyze encounters with the world that occur outside the phenomenological realm of art. The point of this book is to identify, parse, and analyze work related to exhibition and other aesthetic forms that rely not only on sensual engagement inside an exhibition site but also on the cognitive encounters that occur beyond it—most often through reading. The theoretical framework offered by "postsensual aesthetics" takes into account the role of cognition. Ideas move in and through contemporary art, as exhibition extends into publication.

The following proposition, then, seeks to amplify and reposition methodologies by both artists and curators who front knowledge production as something that sidesteps, or runs alongside and at times away from, what is immediately identifiable as art. Therefore, I prefer to take the long perspective on this work. I see it as modes of mediation for public address—as expansive forms of exhibitions and, thus, as modes of curatorial production. The concept of postsensual aesthetics developed herein thus reflects different methodologies of curating that in essence can also provide the conceptual space for different methodologies of art making.

The Curatorial

The field of contemporary art has arrived at forging alliances among disciplines and publishing work in books through a concept and practice called "the curatorial." Maria Lind offered a name to this multifaceted approach to curating in a 2009 essay titled "The Curatorial," inaugurating an *Artforum* column devoted to the field of curating:

> Is there something we could call the curatorial? A way of linking objects, images, processes, people, locations, histories, and discourses in physical space? An endeavor that encourages you to start from the artwork but not stay there, to think with it but also away from and against it? I believe so, and I imagine this mode of curating to operate like an active catalyst, generating twists, turns, and tensions—owing much to site-specific and context-sensitive practices and even more to various traditions of institutional critique.[10]

Lind's proposition for a catalyzing mode of curating is paired in *Artforum* with an analysis of the 28th Bienal de São Paulo in 2008. The exhibition, organized under the title *"in living contact"* by artistic director Ivo Mesquita and curator Ana Paula Cohen, examined the influence that North Atlantic modernism has had over the decades on the shape and character of the Bienal de São Paulo, Latin America's oldest and most important platform for modern and contemporary art. The centerpiece for the curators' self-reflexive institutional critique was the Wanda Svevo Historical Archives, a massive collection of archival materials preserving the history of the Fundação Bienal de São Paulo since its founding in 1951. Cohen and Mesquito invited a significant number of artists who work with archives and collections to participate in the exhibition. Lind combines her reflection on "something" like the curatorial with observations on how the curators sensitively brought complex, research-based work into the public realm. Rather than organizing a physically and visually packed exhibition, they chose to present considerably less artwork than was shown in earlier editions.[11] That decision gave visitors the physical and intellectual space inside the exhibition to experience and contemplate the work. To further assist with the time and attention needed to read and cognitively engage with it, they coordinated several outlets—exhibitions, public programs, and publications—that provided different avenues for arriving at the knowledge recovered by the artists. Lind's argument for these kinds of concerted curatorial strategies underscored the need to take cognition into account as part of the aesthetic experience of work that requires engagement through reading.

Later, in 2011, when asked what she meant by "the curatorial," Lind responded:

> I mean a practice that goes beyond curating, which I see as the technical modality of making art go public in various ways. "Curating" is "business as usual" in terms of putting together an exhibition, organizing a commission, programming a screening series, et cetera. "The curatorial" goes further, implying a methodology that takes art as its starting point but then situates it in relation to specific contexts, times, and questions in order to challenge the status quo. And it does so from various positions, such as that of curator, an editor, an educator, a communications person, and so on. This means that the curatorial can be employed, or performed, by people in a number of different capacities in the ecosystem of art. For me, there is a qualitative difference between curating and the curatorial.[12]

The notion of the curatorial refers to a complicated set of overlapping concerns of cultural production, knowledge production, and audience-building—not to mention entrepreneurship. Curators maintain and draw on vast networks of contacts while managing and organizing an arsenal of resources and tasks, from conceiving and developing ideas for exhibitions, to researching, writing, fundraising, managing, administering, publicizing, hosting, publishing, and archiving. They are responsible for making ideas public and decipherable through processes of mediation, from physical exhibitions and public programs, to online journals and published books. They ultimately need to make convincing arguments for their ideas and propositions. An artistic director and curatorial team for an exhibition on the scale of documenta, or, in Lind's case, leading a contemporary arts institution in a suburb of Stockholm, often have the most personal and professional investment in ensuring that each part of this network of artists, donors, museum administrators, city officials, press—and, of course, audiences—

finds something valuable and at stake in the quality of the work and the attention to how it is presented in the public realm.[13]

By 2018, the interpretation of the curatorial had evolved such that it was defined as a mode of theoretical thinking and research in and of itself. As critic Simon Sheikh reflects,

> The use and indeed usefulness of the curatorial is, then, as an analytical tool and a philosophical proposition, and by indication, a separate form of knowledge production that may actually not involve the curating of exhibitions but, rather, the process of producing knowledge and making curatorial constellations that can be drawn from the historical forms and practices of curating. The curatorial could thus be posited as a form of research, not just into exhibition-making but as a specific mode of research that may or may not take on the spatial and temporal form of an exhibition.[14]

So, as a way of thinking, as Sheikh describes, and working, as Lind details, the notion of the curatorial expands and exceeds traditional curating as a practice through its commitment to pulling together disparate fragments—material and immaterial, conceptual and concrete—into something legible. While the curatorial is more than the traditional concept of curating as a way of making sense of the myriad ideas and information associated with distinct objects, histories, and archives, it nevertheless draws on the characteristics that curation offers for framing assemblages against intellectual, cultural, political, economic, and geographic backdrops. It is comparable, as Lind implied earlier, to the way a conceptual artwork combines archive, form, and content with contemporary life in order to create new knowledge, shifting perspectives of audiences through its "constellation" of elements. It embodies an intention to make something contemporary by situating it in a specific context—spatial, temporal, geographic, racial, historical, social, political—in order to point audiences to what they may find significant in the composition of factors that, on first impression, appear unrelated or discordant from one another.

Knowledge Production and Contemporary Art

The framework of postsensual aesthetics will evolve in this book with and against the curatorial and its tentacular arms of exhibition, where interstitial yet consequential elements constitute meaning. The exhibition as a curatorial concept coalesces through various elements to become an aesthetic form composed of parts that, while themselves individual pieces demanding cognitive engagement beyond the sensual physicality of exhibition, still add to the whole. Audiences, therefore, have both sensual and cognitive encounters with a work dependent on the piece(s) with which they intersect. This expansive and holistic mode of curatorial production uses context against a number of factors—ideas, forms, objects, speculative thought, research, archives—to constitute their contemporaneity. Meanwhile, this mode of production has emerged alongside shifts in the expectations of audiences who have been trained to anticipate that they will learn something from experiencing an exhibition or seeing an object. Tom Holert reflects that by now "regular visitors of contemporary art biennials, modern and contemporary art museums, self-organized art spaces, 'cutting edge' art-school programs, or curatorial-studies summer schools will be much less surprised by the idea that contemporary art is a mode of knowledge production. In fact, they probably cannot think of the practice of contemporary art differently."[15]

This epistemic tendency has increasingly evolved alongside the political motivations assigned to art from modernism, postmodernism, and conceptual art, to what is widely considered contemporary art today, whereas in many cases audiences want to learn. They want to walk away from an exhibition with more knowledge about something than when they entered. And artists and curators want to teach something, often motivated by political, social, economic, and environmental concerns. Curatorial practice as a knowledge-producing field, curator Sofía Hernández Chong Cuy observes, had, by 2013, become "imbued with connotations of political efficacy and a kind mandate to carry out cultural critique; curators were now expected to produce exhibitions and discourses that were somehow alternatives to shows of celebration, spectacle, and populism."[16]

The concept of the curatorial has changed in concert with these conditions and has fueled them. What will become clear as we map a framework for postsensual aesthetics is the intertwined nature of curating, the archive, artistic research, knowledge production, and, particularly, contemporary art. Knowledge production is a fundamental part of the contemporary art industry, as it is in any other information-driven industry in capitalism. Yet this position among other global industries is often a pain point, even perceived as anathema to the ardent perspective that contemporary art is immune to capitalism's influences. Holert observes,

> In its own way, the discipline of art history has long promoted an acknowledgment that works of visual art are sites of epistemological activity. At the same time, however, any too intimate relation of art with knowledge systems and economies has long been deemed suspicious. Knowledge was rarely considered art's major preoccupation, vocation, or end; to the contrary, art has regularly been theoretically framed as radically irreducible to epistemology.[17]

The fact is, however, that the production of knowledge in all of its shapes and forms, from artistic and curatorial research to exhibitions and publications, defines the contemporary art world. Nevertheless, as Holert writes, to date: "Any aesthetic theory centered on art's alleged autonomy refutes identifying art with knowledge."[18]

My formulation and use of the concept of postsensual aesthetics accept that we remain in the aftermath of the ideological aesthetics of art laid down centuries ago, which do not adequately deal with these newer modes of artistic and curatorial production. Still, the term "postsensual aesthetics" should not be mistaken to imply that we are beyond a sensual encounter with art or in the wake of lived, bodily experiences with it. The critique I offer builds on postmodernist criticism on the nature and impact of modernist art and ideologies as they pertain to the object and site of exhibition. It seeks to offer a context for analyzing what changes in artistic and curatorial methodologies represent today in the field of contemporary art. The critical impetus for ideas developed in this book to frame what could be called "postsensualism" is, however, not a repudiation of the sensuality that objects and space possess. Without a doubt, Eichhorn's *documenta 14* exhibition relating to the *Rose Valland Institute*, presented in the Neue Galerie in Kassel, comprised hundreds of artifacts connected to a case study being inventoried at that time by the *Institute*. The objects, such as a tower of books reaching to the ceiling, were real. They had been stolen from their rightful Jewish owners who were killed in the Holocaust. Visitors could experience this work by Eichhorn, see it, walk around it, and be immersed—physically—among the books, art, photographs, and documents.

The artistic and curatorial work we examine, therefore, is inextricably bound to those phenomenological qualities of the exhibition and inherently in conversation with the history of aesthetics informing the field of contemporary art. The exhibition as a physical ground serves some artists and curators as an entry point where visitors can take from that experience whatever knowledge or insight they want or need.[19] Yet this work is more than the objects being presented in an exhibition and is therefore more than what traditional aesthetics can account for. In the "Interlude," we will learn how Adorno drew from what was described as the historical abyss of philosophical discourse to use parts of Kant and Hegel and make them his own. Adorno placed those historical ideas in dialogue with current circumstances in art, culture, and politics in order to create a contemporary theoretical discourse using what could have otherwise been viewed as historical philosophy.

Related to this point, the terms "dialogue" and "contemporary" are used in this book to describe and analyze the work of artists and curators. They constitute the relationships among the components that expose the relevance of a work to its immediate social, political, geographic, and temporal situations. The Middle English *dialoge* comes to us from the Latin via the Greek *dialogos*, which finds its origins in *dialegesthai*, meaning to "converse with." *Dia* meaning "through" unites with *legein*, which means "to speak." We use "contemporary" to convey that something is of one's time. "Contemporary" originates in the mid-seventeenth century from the medieval Latin *contempus*, or *contempor*, composed of *con*, which means "together with," and *tempus*, or *tempor*, which means "time." Something that occurs and lives at the same time is contemporary. Then, "aesthetics" originates from the Greek *aisthesthai*, which means "to perceive," as it relates to human sensation. The German philosopher Alexander Gottlieb Baumgarten appropriated the term for modern usage in the philosophy of art. In his book *Aesthetica* (1750) he offered it as the framework for assessing—or judging—the quality of art's beauty based on the feeling of pleasure or displeasure it gives an individual. While Baumgarten is recognized for introducing "aesthetics" into modern parlance, Kant's formulation of aesthetics in his *Critique of Judgement* (1790) would become the most influential source in philosophy for determining the beauty of an object, a quality inherently subjective as Kant would equate it to the positive or negative stimulation the object has on an individual's senses.[20]

"Dialogue," "contemporary," and "aesthetics" help make sense of the work I examine, whether it be art, exhibitions, or institutions. The theoretical framework of postsensual aesthetics needs these terms and the associative concepts to reflect on the perception of work that is inherently in conversation with a multiplicity of factors that combine to produce knowledge against the backdrop of time and place.

Furthermore, the term "modern" is laced throughout this book. "Modern," from the Latin *modernus*, is also a concept involving time. But, unlike the sense in "contemporary" of being together with one's time, "modern" implies the awareness of an era's relationship to the past. It is associated with the notion of the new, with progress and innovation, a kind of forward motion understood in dialectical relation to the old. History is viewed through the rearview mirror of the present.

The framework of postsensual aesthetics, then, is intended to be a way to capture, amplify, and direct attention to the threads and splinters in artistic and curatorial production that pursue paths divergent from the aesthetics typically associated with art. These paths bring work—research, archives, histories, and ideas—into the public realm through the combination of exhibition and publication using what are strategic and calculated methodologies of curating. They create an active discourse that makes the work contemporary. They do this through the situational structure they impart. And, like Eichhorn's exhibition, the work manifests in different aesthetic forms while withholding the possibility of a total experience in a singular time or place. The intention of this book is to broaden dialogue on the aesthetic dimensions of the exhibition form, potentially issuing new debates on contemporary aesthetics as they relate to these turns from the sensual to the cognitive in contemporary art.

Case Studies

Postsensual Aesthetics is guided by concepts explored in the mid-twentieth-century writings of the Frankfurt School, formally called the Institute for Social Research. Theoretical concepts by Theodor Adorno in particular are appropriated to serve as an organizing framework. Adorno may seem an unlikely bedfellow. But his provocative ideas were fashioned from a productive skepticism of art's capacity to bear the weight of aesthetic ideologies born from the discourse of figures like Kant and Hegel. The principal threads pulled from Adorno's writing twist around each other to make a kind of net intended to hold the theoretical framework that we develop for postsensual aesthetics. To explicate this theory, concepts by Adorno are traced alongside the contours of two exhibitions and one institution: *Documenta11*, directed by Okwui Enwezor, in 2002; *dOCUMENTA (13)*, directed by Carolyn Christov-Bakargiev, in 2012; and the Centre for Contemporary Art Singapore at Nanyang Technological University, founded and directed by Ute Meta Bauer since 2013.[21] The multivalent characteristics of their work, while known to some readers, are analyzed with a pronounced focus on the stewardship of discourse as it relates to their curatorial method ologies. Enwezor's and Christov-Bakargiev's curatorial approaches for their respective editions of documenta represent different yet comparable ways of nurturing alliances among art and other disciplines. Bauer's work at NTU CCA Singapore demonstrates how curatorial methodologies used in exhibitions like documenta can be embedded into the long-term characteristics of an institution's behavior and commitment to research and the epistemological. The curatorial work by Bauer, Christov-Bakargiev, and Enwezor is examined alongside artworks by Maria Thereza Alves, Amy Balkin, Heman Chong, Maria Eichhorn, Claire Pentecost, and Ines

Schaber with the aim of reframing aesthetic forms to account for the liminal, cognitive spaces both inside and outside of the exhibition where aesthetic engagement with art and ideas ultimately transpires.

Postsensual Aesthetics concentrates on these three curatorial projects while shuttling between histories of aesthetic discourse and the evolution of the field of contemporary art. I take this approach to explore how the complex and multifaceted qualities of contemporary curatorial work can, in fact, be seen as symptomatic of much wider and longer retreats from the traditional aesthetics governing the conditions of art, the exhibition, and the institution. What I call an "Interlude" is a discursive excursus that punctuates the sections dedicated to the case studies. The Interlude establishes an introductory history of aesthetic and theoretical discourse, especially as it relates to Adorno's thinking, in order to give all readers a common ground from which this book will draw ideas and against which it reflects on changes occurring in contemporary art. In the spirit of Adorno, the final section, or coda, is simply called "Exact Imagination." This closing section returns to the aesthetic discourses introduced in the Interlude to set them in motion against the propositions, histories, and analyses traced in the earlier sections.

Logic of the Curatorial

In his book *Postproduction* (2002), Nicolas Bourriaud reflects on why he wrote his seminal 1998 work *Relational Aesthetics*.[22] He recounts that he had identified commonalities among a number of artists who, in the 1990s, were using exhibition spaces differently: instead of installing only objects, they created opportunities for spectators to interact by drawing on the social relations among humans as a form—an artistic medium. Bourriaud explains that his writing at the time was an attempt to capture this innovative work and offer a thematic framework and aesthetic criteria for thinking about the common denominators among a group of artists working out comparable questions about what art could be and do. He said that *Relational Aesthetics* was intended to "kick-start" contemporary aesthetics.[23]

More than twenty-five years after Bourriaud wrote his first articles on relational art, the exhibition continues to be an even more formidable factor in the equation for determining what is discussed, understood, and circulated as contemporary art.[24] *Postsensual Aesthetics* intends to contribute to the evolving discourses around these changes in the aesthetics of contemporary art. The artistic and curatorial methodologies traced here offer another reason to pause and contemplate new modes of making work, new modes of producing culture, as they relate to research, knowledge production, and the curatorial. These methodologies have redrawn the boundaries of art and expanded the contours of the contemporary exhibition form that holds it. While the work analyzed in this book is certainly different from relational art, it sits in the same long lineage of artistic and curatorial impulses that pose critical challenges to outmoded aesthetic ideologies. It questions the conditions and logics related to the production of meaning. Still, this focus on knowledge production must be considered with trepidation and skepticism in view of what these changes in the field of contemporary art represent. The work teases with the idea of forgoing categorization, potentially even departing from art. But if that is the case, what does such work mean when looked at alongside other disciplines and fields of research that function solidly as part of cognitive capitalism? That question is underscored throughout the following pages.

Readers, therefore, might recognize connections between this book's subtitle, "On the Logic of the Curatorial," and Rosalind Krauss's "The Cultural Logic of the

Late Capitalist Museum" (1990) (by way of her own citation to Fredric Jameson's 1984 essay "Postmodernism, or the Cultural Logic of Late Capitalism"). Those connections are not without intention. The instrumentalization of artistic research and knowledge production in service to information- and knowledge-based economies is a real concern. Broadening aesthetic criteria raises the risk of relegating contemporary art to a functionary position for cognitive capitalism, adding to the responsibilities already placed upon it to be a spectacular phenomenological experience. The latter is, after all, what Krauss warned of in her incisive critique on the sacrifice of the autonomy of the modernist art object for the ascendency of destination architecture with the makeover of the museum into an arm of the culture industry and mass entertainment. That transformation has become increasingly apparent over the decades, as museum directors have been charged with building a building rather than building a collection, whereas institution building is inherently fused with museum architecture for expanding footprints across the globe. So, while *Postsensual Aesthetics* offers a contemporary aesthetic framework for considering artistic and curatorial methodologies related to knowledge production, it does so with the acute awareness of the undeniable logic of capitalism undergirding so much of the equation. This book is intended, then, to acknowledge these debates and issue new questions about the instrumentalized position of the field of contemporary art and the economic and social factors that continue to shape its ever-evolving character.

Reading through Adorno

Postsensual Aesthetics, like any study, is not comprehensive. My analyses of the two documenta exhibitions, NTU CCA Singapore, and the associative artistic and curatorial drives are not intended to illustrate or corner the work into a singular theoretical reading. These observations are not summary categorizations of these practices. The exhibitions are considered in this context because they possess a wide range of characteristics symptomatic of widespread changes transpiring in contemporary art that arguably signal the emergence of a commitment to new approaches to production deserving of new theoretical frameworks. I am interested, therefore, in identifying and problematizing these conditions in curating and exhibitions, as they can potentially give practitioners better tools to define new paths for making and mediating work, for locating meaning in and through contemporary art.

There are naturally limitations to a writer's capacity to analyze, and a reader's capacity to absorb. This book is intentionally limited in scale with a focused scope. Adorno is our primary interlocutor. Our purpose is not to historicize his writings but to animate them. This is not a philosophical treatise on Adorno. In the spirit of his speculative and experimental thought, I choose to amplify the parts of his writing that help us address some of the questions posed by studying the exhibitions and artworks. My intention is to appropriate Adorno's work in a way that allows us to see why after all these years it resonates for analysis of contemporary art, specifically as we grapple with different methodologies in artistic and curatorial production today. A dogmatic recovery of his theories in this context, anyway, would relegate them to a kind of historical dustbin. We are, I would say, reading through Adorno.

Lastly, while research for this book transpired over a number of years, I began writing it in 2019, one year before the COVID-19 pandemic. As 2020 passed, with blurry anxiety and uncertainty, I worked on this book while thinking about how reading contemporary art applied to the current situation. Millions of people were inside their homes, not attending exhibitions, not visiting museums—not "seeing" art. But they nonetheless continued to engage with the ideas of artists, institutions, and curators. They continued to intersect with art, not through a physical encounter but through a cognitive retreat into the mind. I'm not referring to the numerous galleries and museums that attempted to replicate the ontological experience of the art exhibition by uploading online "viewing rooms." I'm referring instead to the gallerists, curators, and artists who identified the structural form and aesthetic qualities of the digital screen, in this case, to create something that uses the qualities of that form as an opportunity for cognitive engagement with art. At the same time, book sales increased dramatically during the pandemic. Under these conditions, the work of the artists and curators studied in this book became even more electrified and relevant than when I began writing about them.

If the novel coronavirus has taught us anything, it is that there are other ways of doing things, other ways of engaging and relating to each other, caring for each other, and sharing knowledge and ideas beyond the physical public arena. The pandemic hastened and exacerbated many facets of social, political, and urban life that were already fractured and on the verge of radical change. The curatorial methodologies that shape the theoretical framework offered by *Postsensual Aesthetics* may in fact become, in the not-too-distant future, even more pronounced. They could lead to heretofore unknown places and directions in a future that potentially releases art as we know it from the shackles of conventional and outdated aesthetic discourses. This, in turn, could unsettle, or unseat, the behemoth art museums and higher-education institutions that have for decades professionalized art and the attendant artist and curator figures, and which, at this point, are increasingly captive to their own particular sets of outmoded behaviors and ideological expectations. I am optimistic, though, that the methodologies for producing work and inserting it into the public realm pursued by the practitioners studied in this book, combined with the unfortunate era ushered in by the pandemic, have the potential to seed other kinds of aesthetic engagement in and through art—and thus other kinds of relationships between the field of contemporary art, the production of knowledge, capitalism, and our understanding of our world.

Section 1

dOCUMENTA (13)

A State of Mind

On October 25, 2010, Carolyn Christov-Bakargiev wrote a letter to a "dear friend." She tells them she has been traveling for almost two years, moving between urban centers and remote outposts, and meeting with scientists, anthropologists, philosophers, writers, activists, and artists. She ruminates on broad subjects like the power of storytelling, the value of note-taking, and the function of time, while peppering her letter with references to people on a first-name basis: Etel, Bettina, Pierre, Ryan, Theaster, Donna, Lars, Raimundas, Chus, Walid. She asks her "friend" what they are reading. She inquires about their comfort. Musings on the German city of Kassel and its history of manufacturing weapons and locomotives are interlaced with tidbits about the history of the large-scale exhibition documenta, a product of the "trauma" of World War II. She philosophizes on data and information, on the production of knowledge, immaterial laborers, and on capitalism. She closes the letter by sending regrets for her inability to adequately answer the friend's question about the plans and program for *dOCUMENTA (13)*.[1]

Christov-Bakargiev is a curator.[2] The 5,000-word "letter" is a publication produced as part of a series of 100 booklets for *dOCUMENTA (13)*, for which she served as artistic director.[3] The travel she describes was undertaken to organize the exhibition, which opened in Kassel less than two years later, in 2012. The people whose first names she refers to are artists, writers, and curators: Etel Adnan, Bettina Funcke, Pierre Huyghe, Ryan Gander, Theaster Gates, Donna Haraway, Lars Bang Larsen, Raimundas Malašauskas, Chus Martínez, Walid Raad. Her letter, which originally doubled as part of a press release, is not a catalog statement for the exhibition.[4] It is not a formal introduction. Yet it was available over a year in advance of *dOCUMENTA (13)*, so it does something by way of introducing. It reveals process, states the intellectual and creative imperatives, highlights things holding her attention. However, it does not explicitly lay out a plan for the exhibition. It refers to issues that could be things the exhibition will examine, but it does not commit to a theme or concept. It portrays *dOCUMENTA (13)* as "a state of mind."[5]

dOCUMENTA (13) was presented from June 9 to September 16, 2012. In Kassel, the exhibition featured works by 194 participants identified as artists, with installations and programs at ten venues including the Museum Fridericianum, Neue Galerie, Ottoneum Museum of Natural History, Karlsaue Park, and the Kassel Hauptbahnhof.[6] *dOCUMENTA (13)* also occurred, in July, in Alexandria and Cairo with a series of meetings and events involving students from MASS Alexandria along with artists and curators such as Bassam El Baroni, Mai Abu ElDahab, Julie Mehretu, Sarah Rifky, Suely Rolnik, and Wael Shawky. Also in July, *dOCUMENTA (13)* took place in Kabul with a program of seminars and lectures plus an exhibition, which involved artists and critics such as Lara Favaretto, Mariam Ghani, Goshka Macuga, Christoph Menke, Hameed Naweed, Michael Rakowitz, and Mario Garcia Torres. And, in August, *dOCUMENTA (13)* occurred in Banff with a two-week residency involving graduate students and doctoral fellows from the University of Alberta and invited artists, theorists, and curators such as Pierre Huyghe, Raimundas Malašauskas, Chus Martínez, Claire Pentecost, and Kitty Scott.

The geographic dispersal of intense, equally extraordinary, and simultaneous activities and events in five cities and four continents made it difficult to grasp what *dOCUMENTA (13)* was. This activity coincided with an ambitious publication program, including the 100 titles presented in the series called *100 Notes—100 Thoughts*. *dOCUMENTA (13)* featured sixty-six participants from outside the field of art, more than forty of whom contributed to *100 Notes*.[7]

In her letter, Christov-Bakargiev also asks, "What could the word *art* be a stand-in for?"[8] She did not answer that question either—at least not directly. But she did offer a response by curating an edition of documenta whose vast intellectual scope encompassed no less than the history of the universe doubling as an anthology of curatorial practice.[9] It was challenging to comprehend as an exhibition, not to mention impossible to see and experience in totality. And, in fact, Christov-Bakargiev would later remark that she doesn't "even know if *dOCUMENTA (13)* was an exhibition."[10] *dOCUMENTA (13)* was simply unfamiliar and uncategorizable. The complications it posed extended well beyond an obscure press release or the refusal to commit to a theme. But if *dOCUMENTA (13)* was without a concept, it was not without intention or, perhaps more accurately, an attitude. It amounted to an ambitious critique on the scale of troubling the entirety of the institution of documenta, alongside expectations for what a large-scale contemporary art exhibition should look like and what it should do, how it should function, what purpose it should serve, and even when and where it should occur. Furthermore, through its organizational structure and curatorial methodologies, which we will examine, the project problematized the characteristics of artist and curator and researcher and the respective modes of production and expectations associated with each identity. These questions, in turn, lead to thinking about the epistemological crisis of art, or as Christov-Bakargiev asks, "What could the word *art* be a stand-in for?"

I have gone into these details and am interested in *dOCUMENTA (13)* because of the position it took against accepted understandings and interpretations of activity in the field of art, and the conditions that govern them. For our purposes, as I trace a theoretical framework of postsensual aesthetics, *dOCUMENTA (13)* serves as a means to outline how we got here. As an exhibition, it represents the culmination of years of transformation in the field of contemporary art. In this section, our look at *dOCUMENTA (13)* is taken alongside a review of the evolution of curating. The historical and analytical contexts we pull from this review will situate *dOCUMENTA (13)* within a longer trajectory of change in curating whereby knowledge production and research are increasingly brought to the foreground in contemporary art.

Learning from documenta

The curatorial methodologies that Christov-Bakargiev, the *dOCUMENTA (13)* "agents," and participating artists used to realize *dOCUMENTA (13)* originate, in part, in the DNA of the institution.[11] Born from the ravages of World War II, the first documenta occurred in 1955. Originally conceived as a one-time event, *documenta: Art of the Twentieth Century* took up the charge to educate Germany about transformations in modern art.[12] It was organized with the intention of rehabilitating the abstract and expressionist art of the prewar period deemed degenerate by the Nationalist Socialists and reinserting that history into a developing narrative of modern art in Europe and the United States.[13] The exhibition's name derives from the Latin *documentum*, which means "lesson" or "proof," coming from *docere*, meaning "to teach." To that end, documenta was envisioned with a commitment to exhibiting and teaching the "truth of the present."[14] Yet, although the exhibition's goal was to teach about the art of the time, while giving equal attention to science, craft, poetry, literature, industrial design, theater, music, film, and the visual arts, the first *documenta* was also politically motivated to historicize contemporary art in Germany. It was conceived to reposition the nation's cultural output among the advancing innovations in the arts and design in Europe and the United States, thus serving a larger recuperation process of aligning Germany as an equal among other countries in Western Europe.

Arnold Bode, a Kassel-based designer and instructor of exhibition design at the Werkakademie, and Werner Haftmann, a German art historian, were the primary organizers. Haftmann had recently published a survey of modern art titled *Painting in the Twentieth Century*, which became the outline for organizing the first *documenta*.[15] While attempts to forge concrete narratives certainly continued throughout the second half of the twentieth century and Haftmann's book is complicit in that arena, the early editions of documenta under their tutelage signal important shifts in art history. The public-facing power of the contemporary art exhibition begins to wield influence over telling the story of art and, by extension, contemporary art begins writing art history.[16] Moreover, the physical setting of the first *documenta*—situated inside the partially bombed-out interior of the Museum Fridericianum, built in 1779 as the first public museum in Europe—surprisingly morphed the shell of museum architecture into a *Kunsthalle*. The Enlightenment ideal of the museum as promising visitors the knowledge associated with the history and materiality of objects pulled from the ages was exchanged for innovative displays and spectacular juxtapositions offering new contexts and thus new readings to bring audiences up to speed on contemporary twentieth-century art.[17] This turn toward the contemporary exhibition to educate paradoxically marks a turn away from art history as the primary means for learning from art.[18] New ways of seeing and understanding were opened through exhibition-making tactics.

The curatorial models for early editions of documenta tended to synthesize the state of the arts with less interest in claiming a particular instrumental position for them. But things changed in 1972, when the structure shifted from a council-driven model to a single artistic director. *documenta 5*, led by the Swiss curator Harald Szeemann, was organized under the title *Questioning Reality—Pictorial Worlds Today*. The sweeping thematic proposition that Szeemann offered leveled the playing field between "fine art" and what is commonly considered visual culture—consumer goods, media, advertising—drawn from everyday life. Szeemann presented mass-produced objects such as religious tchotchkes and *Der Spiegel* magazine covers in the same exhibition context as work by artists such as Hanne Darboven, Joan Jonas, Yoko Ono, and Paul Thek. Many artists objected. Some, like Robert Morris, withdrew completely from the exhibition, protesting the perceived curatorial overreach. This part of the story of *documenta 5* is well known.[19] The important point is that *documenta 5* was a transitional moment in the history of exhibition making when the curator began to influence how an artwork is made to function in an exhibition and, in some cases, serve as a way for the curator to illustrate a thematic narrative or prove a thesis.

The Rise of the Contemporary Exhibition

Carolyn Christov-Bakargiev's edition of documenta in 2012 draws from and participates in this history of documenta as well as the developing modes of curatorial production witnessed over recent decades. In the 1990s and early 2000s, curating as a field of professional practice in contemporary art advanced rapidly as new perennials—like Manifesta in 1994, the Gwangju Biennale in 1995, and the Guangzhou Triennial in 2002—were launched into the art ecosystem, while their long-established counterparts—namely, the large-scale biennial exhibitions in Venice and São Paulo—gave opportunities to new curatorial perspectives and experiments.[20] The increase in the number of biennials throughout the 1990s was accompanied by more museums and *Kunsthallen* focusing on contemporary art, mounting high-profile thematic exhibitions that drew considerable crowds and prestige. Surging exhibition attendance accompanied by a growing collector base for contemporary art made conditions ripe for the launch of art fairs like the Armory Show in New York in 1994, Art Basel Miami in 2002, and Frieze in London in 2003. The role of the curator as a crucial figure in these arenas, eventually becoming a critical voice in the contemporary art scene, took off. It was not long until higher education stepped into the mix with the founding of graduate programs in curatorial practice, many launching around this time, such as at the Royal College of Art, London, in 1992; the Center for Curatorial Studies, Bard College, in 1994; the Curatorial Program at De Appel, Amsterdam, also in 1994; and at California College of the Arts in 2002.

These changes in curating coincided with greater interest by artists in the temporal and spatial qualities of exhibition and what it could offer as a medium. The increased attention to the exhibition form built upon the legacies of 1970s and '80s collectives such as Group Material and the independently run arts organization Just Above Midtown, which inhabited the institutional framework of curating to exhibit underrepresented work by artists of color. Another important pioneer was artist Martha Rosler, whose work in the 1980s marshaled curatorial tactics that juxtaposed art alongside media, advertising, culture, and politics in order to amplify awareness of urgent issues from the AIDS crisis to homelessness.

By the mid-1990s and early 2000s, as installation and relational art became more visible, the exhibition itself became the mainframe for conceiving new work. Artists whose practices would become loosely grouped under the framework of "relational aesthetics" made exhibitions in close dialogue with curators. Drawing on these histories with the exhibition form while applying innovative curatorial tactics for staging all sorts of ephemeral and time-based activity, curators and artists worked closely to create something, along with the participation of visitors. Curators and artists sometimes worked together to undermine the ingrained effects of art itself, experimenting with new ways of audience solicitation and institutional behavior. At times, it was difficult to distinguish between artist and curator. Many shared a belief in pushing and aggravating the limits of what art is, and who and what could exhibit it, as well as complicating how and when audiences could engage with it. Some of that work evolved by the early 2000s into what was called New Institutionalism, as the same curators moved on to lead institutions and curatorial programs whose core missions were to disrupt the systemic characteristics of art institutions.[21]

dOCUMENTA (13) arrives, in 2012, at what is the tail end of the curator-as-impresario era initiated by Szeemann around the time of *documenta 5*. By the mid-2000s, curating as a complex and vast organism of critical inquiry and creative practice expanded even further and was looked to as a mode of research as much as exhibition making. Critics and curators, such as Beatrice von Bismarck, Dorothee Richter, Irit Rogoff, and Simon Sheikh, whom I quoted earlier, today pursue questions around the epistemological crisis of art, artist, and curator. With the founding of experimental graduate programs—such as the Post-Graduate Program in Curating at Zurich University of the Arts in 2005; Curatorial/Knowledge at Goldsmiths, University of London, in 2006; and Cultures of the Curatorial at the Academy of Fine Arts Leipzig, in 2009—curating has become an expansive field of critical and philosophical inquiry all its own.

These intellectual journeys into the curatorial demonstrate that artistic and curatorial research modalities have the capacity to expose, confound, and trip up the conventional, long-dominant disciplinary apparatuses of art. Wide-reaching modes of production complicate who and what is doing the research, for whom, and to what end or outcome. Yet one of the most prominent through lines in today's take on curating and artistic practice—research—inherently confers the intention to educate, to apply knowledge, and to expose "truth." Some contemporary practitioners, including Christov-Bakargiev, as we shall see, refute the practical application of research, problematizing the market-, institution-, and academic-driven expectations of what an exhibition, artist, and curator should do, their roles, and how they should function (or not).

So, whereas Szeemann looked to the vast range of visual and material production in culture to place alongside fine art in the space of exhibition, Christov-Bakargiev and the agents looked to the vast range of knowledge production across the fields of intellectual, social, historical, and scientific inquiry to ally with art in the space of *dOCUMENTA (13)*. If we think of curating as a kind of stage design—or *mise-en-scène*—one can envision actors and dancers, objects, and materials coming into the exhibition from the field of art, while others enter from "science, including physics and biology, eco-architecture and organic architecture, renewable energy research, philosophy, anthropology, economic and political theory, language and literature studies, including fiction and poetry."[22] *dOCUMENTA (13)* viewed everyone and everything in it as equally crucial to the overall project. Instead of singling out artists in the publications, for example, everyone was grouped together alphabetically as a "participant." In fact, Christov-Bakargiev repeatedly and intentionally used terms like "participant," as well as "worldly," "choreography," and "proposition," in her lexicon around the exhibition, stating,

> I think that right now there is an urgent need for what I call a worldly alliance among so-called cognitive laborers of every sort, artists and scientists and fiction writers and so on. It is very urgent to speak together and to work together and to be in a state of the propositional together. The notion of "the artist" is a very limited notion historically. The ancient Greeks didn't even have a word for "art." They had the word *techné*, which did not at all mean "art" as we understand it today but instead something like "craftsmanship" or "craft." So whether or not art will even continue to be defined as a discrete field for much longer is an open question.[23]

dOCUMENTA (13) also looked to a vast range of objects across centuries and the knowledge associated with their histories and materials. That was most immediately visible to visitors of the ground floor of the Fridericianum where the rotunda was sealed off by glass for what in many ways was the origin story or centerpiece of *dOCUMENTA (13)*: the "Brain." The Brain contained artworks, objects, photographs, and documents—from ancient materials of western Central Asia, to a palette knife used from 1970 to 2011 by the late Lebanese-American Etel Adnan, to a towel and a perfume bottle taken from Hitler's apartment, to a group of three vases that Giorgio Morandi painted during the World War II years. In lieu of a concept, these elements from widely differing eras were combined into a constellation where each object was considered against others and in relation to the totality of the Brain, not to mention the broader characteristics and activities of *dOCUMENTA (13)*. Christov-Bakargiev used to her advantage the visibility, prestige, and history that documenta offers as a formidable institution to complicate some of the accepted tenets defining art, the artist, the exhibition, and the curator. Instead of seeing the museum as a space to legitimize the value of work, as Szeemann perhaps did, she viewed the entire field of contemporary art as a massive, unifying crucible where research and knowledge production could coalesce, potentially shedding preconceived outcomes.

Yet, while the production, distribution, and consumption of knowledge are detectable concerns, these were not declared themes for the exhibition. In fact, Carolyn Christov-Bakargiev and the curatorial team adamantly believed that an overarching concept would instrumentalize the artwork, placing it in service to a curatorial conceit.[24] Their refusal to provide a thematic framework prevented a definite conclusion from being reached. A conclusion attempting to illustrate a position (as Szeemann did) would have signaled the intention to prove a thesis and therefore produce some kind of knowledge toward an ultimate end, which, for Christov-Bakargiev, would in turn have put the exhibition and the artworks into an even greater instrumentalized role, potentially situating them alongside other research fields of cognitive capitalism. The exhibition, in that case, would have been one more cultural enterprise contributing to the immaterial labor economy, consequently succumbing to the notion that a contemporary art exhibition should pursue and offer conclusive statements on issues and answers to problems as part of its function in capitalism. *dOCUMENTA (13)* was, instead, more *of* than *about*. It was an attitude, or, as Christov-Bakargiev wrote, "a state of mind."

Aesthetic Regimes of Art

Still, incoherence and indeterminacy aligned with a state of mind are not always welcome qualities in contemporary art exhibitions. In a 2015 essay titled "Curating against the Apocalypse, *Documenta 13*, 2012," the art historian T. J. Demos writes about works in *dOCUMENTA (13)* that explored land use, energy sources, ecology, and environmental activism. In this expanded version of a 2012 review for *The Brooklyn Rail*, he reflects on works by artists Song Dong, Moon Kyungwon and Jeon Joonho, Christian Philipp Müller, The Otolith Group, and Claire Pentecost within the context of the exhibition's detectable, yet in no way explicit, thematic commitment to the environment:

> Described somewhat cunningly as "an exhibition without a concept" by Christov-Bakargiev in the run-up to the show—in order to de-instrumentalize and singularize the inclusions, visitors were told—*Documenta 13* largely outsourced the definition of the show's conceptualization to its impossibly multiple and at times internally conflicted *100 Notes—100 Thoughts* series. While this overwhelming panoply provided little immediate service to visitors at the exhibition, the publications do open up fertile territory for considering the pressing environmental matters raised in the exhibition, even while these matters were never explicitly identified or linked to the show's individual artistic contributions.[25]

Demos refers to the *100 Notes* series, which, as mentioned, was integral to the overall curatorial methodologies of *dOCUMENTA (13)*. Produced and commissioned by Christov-Bakargiev and the curator and art historian Chus Martínez, and managed by editor Bettina Funcke, the booklets were distributed on a staggered schedule beginning about a year in advance of the opening in Kassel. Numbered individually from 001 to 100, the series was designed by the Milan-based Leftloft with distinctively coordinated colors, paper quality, and three different formats (A6, A5, B5).[26] Names are boldly printed on the covers in a typeface called Glyph. Contributors ranged from contemporary artists, curators, and art historians, such as Etel Adnan, Alanna Heiss, Emily Jacir, Pamela M. Lee, Issa Samb, Jalal Toufic, Ian Wallace, and Lawrence Weiner, to names less familiar to the field: Karen Barad, Susan Buck-Morss, George

Chan, Ashraf Ghani, Donna Haraway, Sonallah Ibrahim, Vandana Shiva, and Michael Taussig. Some booklets have text and illustrations, others communicate using graphs and drawings. Some content is pulled from facsimiles of existing archival works or out-of-print publications. In many cases, newly commissioned criticism and personal reflections are published. The topics range from poetry, architecture, and theory, to urban planning, quantum physics, hospitality, and politically engaged literature. Photographic-based contributions sit alongside booklets about postcolonialism and love. Some booklets relate directly to the sites of *dOCUMENTA (13)*—Banff, Cairo, Kabul—while others deeply engage with the history of documenta in Kassel. The list goes on. With the underlying concept of the "note," they amplify the value of process, acts of openly thinking through something, recording documentations and artifacts, holding fragments and unfinished thoughts. They are different modalities for drawing connections between the private and public processes of doing, providing insight into different methods of making and thinking. In this sense, they are unassuming forms of showing ideas in a state of becoming.[27] *100 Notes—100 Thoughts* is dispersed across the world, available at commercial and independent outlets, and continues to be a decidedly visible and accessible part of *dOCUMENTA (13)*.

Christov-Bakargiev's "Letter to a Friend," which is booklet No. 003, embodies this ethos of thinking through in real time what something—like an edition of documenta—is and can be. Christov-Bakargiev continues,

> This reminds me that I must tell you about the notebooks that we will publish. Yes, a hundred little pieces of bound paper in various sizes that Bettina [Funcke] is carefully overseeing and bringing together. As a prelude to the 2012 exhibition, they will start to appear next year, in 2011. Note-taking encompasses witnessing, drawing, writing, and diagrammatic thinking; it is speculative, manifests a preliminary moment, a passage, and acts as a memory aid or trace. With contributions by authors from a range of disciplines, such

> as art, science, philosophy and psychology, anthropology, economic and political theory, language and literature studies, as well as poetry, *100 Notes—100 Thoughts* constitutes a space of *dOCUMENTA (13)* to explore how thinking emerges and lies at the heart of reimagining the world.[28]

T. J. Demos is one of the few critics who focused most thoroughly on the *100 Notes* series. Yet his reflection offers a chance to examine how criticism serves as a kind of border control for keeping intact expectations for what an exhibition is. We can situate this criticism within an aesthetics that governs what art and exhibitions are presumed to look like and how they can be expected to function. Demos is a distinguished art historian and curator with a highly influential voice in contemporary art, whose writing appears in respected journals and numerous publications. His criticism thus affects the judgment of artistic and curatorial practices. These practices are conceived, developed, and pursued within the historical trajectory, or the "regime," of the aesthetics of art. Added to these conditions are the current pressures that art be critical. As mentioned earlier, regarding Hernández Chong Cuy's and Holert's observations, the field of contemporary art today is generally considered a site of knowledge production that provides solutions to real-world problems or at the very least addresses them head on. The work of artists and curators who pursue long-term research and seek multiple avenues for public presentation often becomes functionalized because of the shady area between criticality and contemporary art, whereas Demos writes, "In the present age of crises and emergencies, we need bold proposals, not the fuzzy rejection of guiding concepts."[29] This is the logic of contemporary art.

On one hand, we could argue that art and exhibition cannot and should not be responsible for doing it all. Still, Christian Philipp Müller, The Otolith Group, and Claire Pentecost, whom Demos singles out, seek to use their work in some cases to make a tangible impact. Many of them collaborate with practitioners outside of art, sometimes literalizing and functionalizing the work with an intention to instigate change. On the other hand, Pentecost's vertical beams filled with soil and sited in the gardens of the Ottoneum, for example, were too aestheticized for Demos. They intermingled too inconspicuously with the garden environment outside the Ottoneum to fulfill their function as functional contemporary art. They looked like art. Their pleasing adornment of the gardens, for Demos, was a missed opportunity for "the radical nature of her creations, meant as prototypes for self-sufficient food production in gardenless urban areas, as well as conceptual proposals for delinking arable land from commercial property—that is, unless one was already familiar with the artist's politico-ecological commitments."[30]

Demos found it necessary to have obvious connections, from an identifiable concept informing viewers what to expect and how the exhibition would perform, to a decipherable correlation between the writing in *100 Notes—100 Thoughts* and the art in the exhibition. In his view, the curating did not adequately service the issues that the exhibition raised: "While *Documenta 13* can be credited with opening up ecological discourse in productive ways and confronting visitors with a variety of positions, it also exemplifies the failure to do anything about the very issues it raised—as if mere knowledge production releases us from any responsibility for doing things differently at the curatorial level."[31]

A Kind of Fugitive Art

The exhibition as a form of public address can and often does provide an introduction to work like Pentecost's where audiences inevitably need to read more before or after seeing it in order to advance the information-driven component of the art. Audiences need to follow some artists. Pentecost's practice draws on other disciplines and reaches the public realm through a variety of outlets, including books and other routes of knowledge production like talks and panels. Audiences have an opportunity to read texts about her work, some of them integrated parts of projects, such as No. 061, "Notes from the Underground," in *100 Notes*. And, as Demos observes in his analysis of her work, it is helpful to have a sense of her commitments, a primer about the work.

Yet anyone attending *dOCUMENTA (13)*, or, for that matter, numerous other exhibitions, would be unable to make the connection on the spot to the functional objectives or the deeply integrated and largely invisible modes of collaboration in Pentecost's practice. In that physical moment in the Ottoneum gardens, they would not have known that the vertical growing systems were a collaboration between Pentecost and the designer and philanthropist Ben Friton of the nonprofit urban-gardening organization Can YA Love. Friton and Pentecost conceived the vertical gardens, in part, to prototype possible solutions to areas with limited soil and land resources in Nairobi, Kenya. In Kassel, three vertical beams were sited near the Ottoneum, each operative in a different but complementary capacity. One column provided vegetables for the nearby food kiosk operated by the artist-run initiative AND AND AND; a second column was used to grow legumes in order to produce nutrient-rich soil as part of the symbiotic exchange among carbohydrates, bacteria, and nitrogen necessary for the production of healthy soil; and flowers were planted in a third column to support the work of bees and other pollinators.[32] Together, the three columns represented the complex composition of the garden ecosystem. Several additional columns were sited around Kassel and used as community gardens for vegetable growing and composting.

So, rather than faulting the exhibition or the display of a work for not fulfilling the expectations that govern the moment of encounter, we might reconsider the aesthetics that have come to regulate the analysis of this kind of work and, instead, consider the many points available for entering it—the physical art exhibition being only one way. Work like this needs to be assessed over longer temporal continuums, taking into account the various ways they manifest in public—exhibitions, books, talks—and within the artist's overall practice. If not, we continue to burden art with established ideologies to perform as art in the very moment of its reception in an exhibition. The complexity of some art cannot fully reach audiences only through an exhibition, within a single, perceptual moment of engagement. In work like Pentecost's, which utilizes many modes of distribution and reception, we could interpret the momentary materialization in the public realm through an exhibition or a book as one fragment within a much larger composition. Then we could consider how that fragment operates as part of the entirety of the whole.

In the case of Pentecost's contribution to *dOCUMENTA (13)*, the vertical soil beams were part of an overall cosmology, or constellation, of a larger body of work called *soil-erg*. The beams complemented an exhibition of work inside the Ottoneum that included the presentation of sculptural forms resembling ingots, large discs made of organic matter, and more than forty drawings taking the form of oversized paper currency. These drawings depicted humans recognized for outstanding achievements in agricultural science as well as nonhumans, such as snails, bees, and microorganisms, that make equally important contributions to a healthy, functioning environment. Here, too, was an eighteenth-century cabinet pulled from the museum's collection that houses the oldest geological sample from Hesse, an area in central Germany. The artist made a replica of the cabinet and placed her copy next to the original. Inside the replicated cabinet, she created the conditions for a composting bed where worms fed on kitchen scraps provided over the 100 days of *dOCUMENTA (13)*.

Small microphones inserted into this soil-making machine amplified the sounds of busy worms manufacturing nourishing soil. Visitors could hear them working as they experienced the other components of Pentecost's exhibition.

Another factor to consider in understanding the larger composition of a work is the outside expertise coming into art to contribute to the work. Pentecost and Christian Philipp Müller both collaborated with scientists and administrators from the Faculty of Organic Agricultural Sciences at the University of Kassel. In fact, quite a few artists participating in *dOCUMENTA (13)* made projects in collaboration or partnership with people typically operating outside the field of art. William Kentridge worked with the Harvard University historian and philosopher of science Peter L. Galison to realize Kentridge's *The Refusal of Time.*[33] Ines Schaber collaborated with the writer and social theorist Avery F. Gordon to make *The Workhouse: Room 2*. That project examined the long, troubled history of Breitenau. Originally built as a monastery in 1874, located about three miles south of Kassel, Breitenau later served as a labor house and correctional facility. Around 1933, in the early days of the Nazi era, the facility became a concentration camp for political prisoners. Schaber's project for *dOCUMENTA (13)* contributed to her ongoing series examining the relationship between architecture, power, and bodies of knowledge, which she has pursued since 2010 with Gordon, a sociologist based at the University of California, Santa Barbara, whose research centers on captivity and war. Gordon's notebook, No. 041, "Notes for the Breitenau Room of *The Workhouse,*" offers an annotated timeline of the history of trauma at Breitenau. In the installation at *dOCUMENTA (13)*, archival photographs of various protagonists in Breitenau's history were drawn from the archives, altered, and arranged into a narrative that directed attention to the problematic past of the building. Other artists collaborated with indigenous people, as Maria Thereza

Alves did in constructing something called *chinampas*—artificial islands—in a lake in Mexico. The project used indigenous engineering practices to address the deteriorating water resources. She presented documentation of this project and published a completely separate book about it as part of her exhibition contribution to *dOCUMENTA (13)*.[34]

Some artists tied their work directly to the administrative and financial resources of art institutions. Khaled Hourani organized the loan of a painting by Picasso to Ramallah with the assistance and indemnifying support of the Van Abbemuseum in Eindhoven. As a result, he arranged for the exhibition of a work by Picasso for the very first time in the unrecognized state of Palestine. In a comparable vein, Amy Balkin also collaborated with an institution, in this case *dOCUMENTA (13)*, to help with an ambitious multipronged global project called *Public Smog*. Since 2004, Balkin has worked with *Public Smog* to draw attention to the tangled intersections of climate change, bodily wellbeing, industrial capitalism, and geopolitics by pursuing a seemingly impossible task of opening a clean-air park in Earth's atmosphere. In June 2004, she launched what is called the "Lower Park" in an area of the sky over Los Angeles, Orange, and Riverside counties in California. Governed by the South Coast Air Quality Management District, Balkin opened the park by purchasing credits to offset smog-producing emissions of nitrogen oxides (NO_x). Nitrogen oxides are the gases responsible for polluting the tropospheric zone, the lowest layer of the atmosphere where poor air quality with fine particulates directly impact individuals, causing long-term health issues like asthma and lung disease. The park was open above that area until the offsets expired, two weeks after their purchase.[35] *Public Smog* fluctuates in location and duration, dependent on where and how much is paid for offsets.

In 2006, Balkin worked with the Royal College of Art's curatorial program. The college provided an artist stipend and funding to purchase offsets through the European Union Emissions Trading Scheme. This time, carbon dioxide credits (CO_2) were purchased to open an "Upper Park" in the stratosphere. The condition of this higher layer of atmosphere has more sweeping consequences impacting the long-term health of planetary life—oceans, glaciers, plants, animals, humans—through climate change. Also in 2006, Balkin called and wrote officials at the United Nations Educational, Scientific and Cultural Organization (UNESCO) to inquire about the process for adding the atmosphere to UNESCO's World Heritage List. She learned that typically one of the State Parties, or member nations, must nominate a site for inscription to the list. However, in this case, since all State Parties are impacted by the quality of the atmosphere, all 186 member nations must agree on the universal value of the atmosphere and that its conservation essential.

Open or closed, in reality and concept, the park relies on many outside advisors on clean air, including atmospheric chemists, climate scientists, UNESCO World Heritage policy specialists, emissions traders, and activists. The borderless project became simultaneously an exercise in statecraft, a defense of the atmosphere as public commons, and a critique of the monetization of emissions—pollution—as a new form of libidinal capitalism in the unrequited promise of market-based mechanisms to slow carbon emissions. Nevertheless, with no official government sponsor to nominate Earth's atmosphere for protection under UNESCO, the case for *Public Smog* was left at that.

Around 2010, *Public Smog* took a turn that signaled a potentially more systemic solution. The impossibility of nominating *Public Smog* to UNESCO pursued four years earlier became possible with Balkin's participation in *dOCUMENTA (13)*. The exhibition renewed attempts to add the atmosphere to sites protected by the UNESCO World Heritage Convention. Marshaling the bureaucratic resources and state recognition of *dOCUMENTA (13)* as a political entity, Balkin and Christov-Bakargiev solicited nominating support from member nations to expand the clean-air park from piecemeal offset purchases constrained to time and place to the entirety of Earth's atmosphere. After Germany rejected a request to act as lead State Party, Christov-Bakargiev on behalf of *dOCUMENTA (13)* and *Public Smog* sent 186 letters to member nations. Arguing that conserving the atmosphere was by extension in the best interest of conserving every nation's heritage through human continuity, she appealed to each and every State Party to lead a coalition to inscribe the atmosphere in the list of protected sites.[36] Thirteen offices responded. All declined to support the effort except the Kingdom of Tonga, which expressed interest in the proposal but lacked the resources.

It is not uncommon for artists to rely on the expertise of others to make things for them. One can think of any number of artists, such as Carol Bove, Jeff Koons, Simone Leigh, and Danh Vo, who have work fabricated by a team of experts. But the above-mentioned works by artists participating in *dOCUMENTA (13)* such as Balkin and Pentecost represent a kind of fugitive art, work that boomerangs from the field of art to siphon the knowledge of other fields, get the expertise it needs, and then bring it back as an integral part of presenting work in the public realm. The immaterial contributions by experts, bureaucrats, and even politicians, while technical and circumstantial, are usually undetectable in the final presentation of the work. Yet their contributions routinely become visible in printed matter or other kinds of texts published as part of exhibitions and in books. In the Museum Fridericianum, Balkin presented framed copies of all of the letters written by Christov-Bakargiev to member nations and the thirteen replies. The installation also included a station with postcards inviting visitors to support the effort by adding their name to the petition to preserve Earth's atmosphere as an important part of the world's cultural and national heritage.[37] Two copies of a behemoth book—over 700 pages—with the administrative documents and letters, applications, written arguments, and justifications for the universal values connected to the project were also available to visitors.

Balkin's work is complex. It requires reading and thinking. It requires more time than one can reasonably give to it in an exhibition. But the difference between work by Balkin and by someone like Koons is that the latter's work is experienced in totality inside an exhibition. That moment is it. That's all. Audiences do not need to know anything before or after seeing it in order to have a total aesthetic experience with Koons's art. Work by Balkin or Pentecost, on the other hand, not only relies on the considerable knowledge of people outside of the art field to make it, but also encourages audiences to come prepared with knowledge in order to get something more from it.[38] Or, it requires them to take more time inside the exhibition to read the breadth of research and content presented. From 2006 to 2021, *Public Smog* had an entire website providing digital access to a bevy of documents, administrative applications, excerpts from transcripts of phone calls, and letters related to research, negotiation, and administrative processes inherent to the work. All of this was made available to the public; it was conceived as being integral to the work. Another component is a twenty-minute, standalone video installation that presents these materials when the work is shown in an exhibition context. As for Pentecost's *soil-erg*, Demos rightly reads her soil beams as prototypes, literal steps in a process to advance food production in land-poor areas. The writer knew about the prototype when remarking on the work. He, like others, would not have gathered information about it from only seeing—phenomenologically experiencing—the sculptures installed in the Ottoneum gardens.

Audiences, consequently, must read more in order to have a better sense of what some artists' projects that rely on research and intentionally incorporate text are all about. Reading has an incredibly important function for these kinds of work, not only inside the space of an exhibition but beyond it, cognitively connecting to audiences who are physically somewhere else. *100 Notes* addressed this need to a certain extent. That's why the series appeals to critics, such as Demos, who advocate for a more transparent approach to knowledge production through art. But, as we have discussed, this tactic falls prey to what is increasingly and more generally expected of contemporary art. The books, indeed, are one way to satisfy audiences' desire for literal information. They are also an effective way to aestheticize the otherwise buried work by figures whose contributions could remain invisible. We should not, in other words, consider this kind of work within such limited, existing parameters of art but, instead, step outside ideologies ingrained by figures like Kant, Hegel, and Adorno. We will look at these figures in the following pages, and see how the characteristics of contemporary work are representative of a larger and longer transitional period moving away from the governing aesthetics they laid ground for.

Artistic Research

The outside voices and books incorporated into the work of contemporary practitioners, by most accounts, are expected to produce some kind of knowledge. It doesn't matter whether or not the knowledge has a function. It exists. And contrary to what Christov-Bakargiev may have intended with *dOCUMENTA (13)*, people will use it as they wish. But, to Christov-Bakargiev's point, the field of contemporary art needs to be careful not to become another knowledge-producing agent for capitalism, which is the potential pitfall it faces by aligning the production of knowledge vis-à-vis "artistic research" too closely to the systemic infrastructures of university and corporate organization and funding. This alignment can be interpreted as a means toward perceived legitimacy by promising the production of truth and meaning equal to the way the natural sciences, social sciences, technology, and engineering function within a neoliberal research university.[39] The theorist Dieter Mersch, whose work investigates the aesthetic dimensions of theory as it relates to contemporary art, addresses the question,

> *What is the basis of art's specific form of knowing?*, the answer is that it does not consist in the increase of positive knowledge about the world, which may in turn be affirmed or denied, i.e. whose truth or falsehood is in question—the purpose of the arts is not to explain, but rather *to open up new dimensions* which evoke *reflexive knowledge which could not otherwise be gained*. And that ultimately means that aesthetic or artistic knowledge is closer to the nature of philosophical knowledge than scientific knowledge.[40]

For some practitioners and critics, the curatorial as a mode of research is a way of pursuing a totalizing approach to meaning-making wherein knowledge in and of itself becomes the event.[41] For others, the research is a rehearsal of doubt, or disbelief, in art's continued relevance. They push against the contours of meaning, looking to the etymological roots of "research"—more akin to the Greek *sképsis*, which means "search." The skeptic, in fact, may be thought of as someone who searches for truth—in knowledge—by mentally suspending preexisting beliefs in order to identify a greater level of awareness and understanding about objects, ideas, history, and reason.[42] Some curatorial methodologies, like those used for *dOCUMENTA (13)*, give agency to audiences to do something with the elements of information, material, history, and archive. They can order the points into a constellation legible to them. Agency is thus an important part of the equation. Yet figures such as Maria Eichhorn remain obstinate that they do not expect audiences to do anything with the information. Eichhorn uncovers and frames the facts "because people should be aware of these things."[43] These aesthetic frameworks by curators and artists do not necessarily tell audiences what to think, or provide a tidy conclusion, as much as they give contexts and tools to piece together knowledge using whatever means relevant and at hand. In doing so, the curatorial methodologies are closer to Mersch's statement that aesthetic knowledge is on par with philosophical knowledge, as opposed to the kind of truth sought by the sciences.[44]

It is, indeed, possible to give audiences agency using this formation of "curatorial constellations," to quote Simon Sheikh again. The constellation modality speaks to the work of Christov-Bakargiev for *dOCUMENTA (13)*, as well as to what we will see in the work by Okwui Enwezor and by Ute Meta Bauer. They each push against the contours of the exhibition to stretch and expand them, showing us how the exhibition as a thing can be more than a presentation of material objects in physical space. Christov-Bakargiev reminds her "dear friend," in the same letter, that little more than a decade after documenta's founding, by the late 1960s, "the exhibition itself (its concept, its sites, its installation) became the object of the exhibition."[45] The exhibition form, in other words, is the central force for staging experiences with art where ideas and knowledge are born from context, not necessarily from isolated, singular art objects. These contemporary exhibition methodologies construe meaning from the nodal elements when brought into dialogue with the spatial and temporal situations in which those elements are presented, be it an exhibition or not. The curatorial, then, is contemporaneity, whereas the methodologies are forms of research committed to uncovering, or recovering, why something (or a combination of things) should matter to an audience, whether museumgoers, readers, students—or anyone.

The exhibition, as a conceptual framework—as a thing—could thus be seen as a form of research and proposition, made through alliances across the disciplinary spectrum, that is opposed to the ingrained histories and understandings of art.[46] The complications posed by the organization of *dOCUMENTA (13)* are characteristic of a turn in contemporary art where it has become increasingly common for collaborators from other fields to step into art to make work in and through exhibition. This turn is accompanied by the extension of audience engagement beyond the temporal and spatial parameters of exhibition, or the traditional spaces of art, into other forms, such as the booklets published for *dOCUMENTA (13)*. The cognitive, conceptual context of curating provides the crucial frame for these shifts, and it does so, increasingly, to a greater extent than the physical exhibition itself.

In theory and practice, Christov-Bakargiev makes a case for the curatorial as a constructive form of cultural production that activates art—and, actually, anything and anyone—in order to make them contemporary. The postsensual theoretical framework we are developing seeks to amplify this activity in contemporary art as symptomatic of changing characteristics in the aesthetic dimensions of the exhibition. Postsensualism is responsive to curatorial practices that expand the spatial and temporal qualities of the exhibition form by composing an exhibition from strategically coordinated elements that refuse to allow the physical site to be the primary point of contact, thus requiring cognitive engagement beyond it. The works examined here are only a few examples of the extraordinary number operating in this manner. For this reason, a theoretical framework like postsensual aesthetics is helpful for describing and analyzing them, and thinking about these modes of production as increasingly influential threads in contemporary art.

The Follower: Later and Somewhere Else

I want to take the concept of the curatorial further by looking at its most salient component: the audience—or the experiencing subject. The subject is crucial in the overall combined factors that influence aesthetic experience. Knowing something in advance of seeing a work by artists such as Balkin, Eichhorn, and Pentecost can be beneficial to the reception of their work. As we learned from Demos, if one comes to Pentecost's soil beams with the information that they are prototypes for part of a larger project, that awareness informs the experience of her work in the gardens in Kassel. This awareness is knowledge, gained by reading something integral to the work. Earlier, I mentioned that audiences might need to follow artists. The term "follower," which is often applied to social media users, pertains to how people know about and engage with work by some artists and curators. Followers are accustomed to consuming fragments of culture. Followers burrow into successive hyperlinks on the screen of a laptop. They scroll through social media posts on an iPhone, subscribe to video channels, read books and magazines, view exhibitions, and attend public programs. They gather and decipher meaning in the images and ideas coming at them from mediated sources. They piece together information to construct a narrative about a specific person, event, or current issue. That narrative is personalized, specific to them and the sources at hand. But that narrative is always partial. They do not have the entire story. These are the realities of contemporary life. Fragmentation is a recognizable form.

Contemporary art and exhibitions are part of the realities of how pieces of information—fragments—are consumed and transformed into knowledge and understanding. The follower profile applies to exhibitions where visitors might be thrown into what feels like an existing conversation with an artist, a curator, or an institution because they encounter and experience what is sometimes only part of an ongoing project. On entering the *Rose Valland Institute* at *documenta 14*, one would have no idea that the towering display of books alongside the artifacts being cataloged were necessarily part of a much larger organism. Visitors might be introduced to the *Institute* there, and then take that awareness and learn more later. Furthermore, while the experiencing subject might have difficulty staying with a prolonged argument in one sitting—whether made in writing, through film or video, a photographic essay, online, or in the physical space of exhibition—audiences are increasingly comfortable with absorbing parts of intellectual, visual, and creative content and then moving on. They know they can read (or watch) more later. Just as when using social media, they can arrange the pieces in ways that potentially transform complex ideas and theories into a personal interpretation of the work before them.

In cases where printed matter and other published material are integrated into curatorial methodologies, the resulting exhibition as a form becomes elastic by functioning across temporal and spatial frameworks. This elasticity provides open access to the work and the knowledge it imparts, impacting how the experiencing subject views and relates to the overall project of an artist or a curator. The conventional interpretation of time as a linear concept, at least as far as what an exhibition experience is conceived to be, becomes less relevant for getting at meaning. That open access is often provided by printed books and online content strategically conceived as components that complement and extend the work away from the physical constraints of exhibition into the "anytime-anywhere." Whether they are newly introduced or seasoned followers, experiencing subjects are given the option to take the exhibition encounter from the public realm to the private home, to experience the work on their own terms—later and somewhere else.

While some artists and curators are continually working with models that mime how contemporary audiences connect to content in everyday life, the institution of art has difficulty pulling together and analyzing dispersed or atomized forms of public address. Artists and curators whose work I examine in this book understand how to inhabit and use the form of fragmentation to their advantage. Yet, recognizing the breathtaking scope and scale of *dOCUMENTA (13)*, we can see that a certain degree of imagination was, indeed, necessary for piecing together the various components that audiences would have been aware of but unable to access. The exhibition essentially refuted itself, denying audiences the opportunity to have a total experience. It was simply impossible to see as a thing, with different elements happening simultaneously in vastly different geographic regions. The institutional blind spot for this curatorial work, however, is telling in critics' reviews of *dOCUMENTA (13)*.[47] A lot of the criticism of the exhibition briefly acknowledged the *100 Notes* series, but there was scant assessment or interest in talking critically about these publications as essential to the exhibition. With few exceptions, the booklets are mostly discussed in interviews and public talks by Christov-Bakargiev and Bettina Funcke.[48] T. J. Demos's review, as I mentioned, dealt most concretely with the publication component. Nevertheless, the questions posed by critics about how to make sense of it all are valid. If audiences encounter a cross-section of a larger project, taken at any given moment from any different point of view—from social media, physical exhibits and publications, to talks and performances—what, then, is the work of art (or exhibition), who is the artist (or curator), and against which aesthetic criteria are they understood?

Ideological Fissures

This question returns us to the questions posed earlier related to the singularity of the artist figure—a persona imbued with and belabored by the behavioral characteristics that history has granted to the performance of being an artist. While artists like Carol Bove, Jeff Koons, Simone Leigh, and Danh Vo outsource the fabrication of works, the notion of creative vision remains intrinsically tied to an awareness of the artist as an individual. Names of fabricators are not routinely visible. By contrast, other artists, such as Maria Thereza Alves, Amy Balkin, Maria Eichhorn, Claire Pentecost, and Ines Schaber, who rely on organizations and experts for knowledge of such things as materials, administration, legal processes, and archival histories, often make public the names of collaborators as an ordinary part of the process of exhibition making. These artists at times take advantage of the generous space of contemporary art to sidestep the singularity of the artist figure in exchange for nurturing alliances among knowledge producers, while using the multifaceted qualities of the contemporary art exhibition as an essential way to mobilize and operationalize those alliances. While they make these contributors visible, this is not to say that the identity of these artists does not stand with the locus of the work; it does. But the acknowledgment of the names of people, organizations, and agencies who contribute to the work as part of the aesthetic form, not to mention the publication of research and writing in relation to it, signals something like a fissure in the ideological singularity of the artist figure that has come down to us through the ideological constraints governing art. This public recognition of contributors explores the otherwise hidden processes of negotiation, administration, and research integral to the work.

The division of intellectual and creative labor found in these modes of artistic production runs counter to the established idea of the artist as an isolated and autonomous figure. That impression is increasingly perceived to be antiquated. But the reality is that the artist, as a professional practitioner, is still known to require a studio and uninterrupted time to make work, and usually to prefer to be alone while working. It is instilled in us that the nature of the artist's practice demands it. The notion of artistic practice largely remains defined by the production of material artwork with the intention to eventually present it in a physical exhibition. The making process that encompasses research—work that does not culminate in material results—is not typically considered part of artistic practice or at least is something that does not have an aesthetic equivalent. In other words, research is not readily representable. The proliferation and idolization of the artist residency in contemporary art reinforces the idea of the practicing artist, someone who needs a place to create work, a kind of genius figure removed from the bustle and distraction of everyday life to focus on the material-making process. The prized individual graduate studio in an arts academy, too, systemically sets up from an early stage of development the ideal of an artist as someone who needs isolated physical space to create—objects. The immaterial production of knowledge and research simply does not figure into the impression of what it means to be a practicing artist.

This notion of the artist as an exceptional genius can be traced, in part, to Kant. In his *Critique of Judgement* (1790), which we consider in the Interlude, Kant contrasts the artist with a scientist, someone who assembles and identifies different parts and pieces of logical steps toward proving a hypothesis. The scientific process is teachable, as the discipline is based on identifiable procedures. Artists, on the other hand, do not necessarily follow logical procedures in the processes of work. Their work originates from ideas and skills that are natural to the talents and experiences of the individual artist and, therefore, are not teachable. As with Kant's philosophy on the experience of art, the talent of the artist is entirely tethered to nature.[49]

Logic of Disintegration

The curatorial methodologies used to organize *dOCUMENTA (13)* are incremental steps to reconciling the impossible positions, tasks, and limitations history has placed on art. The expectations are based on the ideals associated with being art and, by extension, being artist. The problem with this dialectical thinking is the continual policing of the ideals—like these very concepts of art and artist, as described above. What originates from supposedly rational thinking associated with ideals can morph into universalisms, such as fascism, communism, democracy, and capitalism. Society exists each day in the abyss of ideological constructs. The concept of the constellation, where the particular becomes paramount, is key to thwarting the impact of ideological thinking, instead allowing identification of "individual elements" in different configurations and therefore different interpretations. Nothing is fixed.[50]

The curatorial methodologies pursued by Christov-Bakargiev and the *dOCUMENTA (13)* agents privileged the threads and fragments—the unfinished theses and inconclusive concepts—over the offering of a foregone conclusion or even conceding that the exhibition should look like exhibition. *dOCUMENTA (13)* performed, to some degree, a position antithetical to both identity and ideology because it was so patently unrecognizable. Its contours and lines were organic and, as I mentioned, not *about* something but *of* it. One need only page through *dOCUMENTA (13)*'s main catalog, *The Book of Books*, where almost all of the *100 Notes* are compiled and reproduced, to have a sense of a living body in motion.[51] The breadth of subjects covered becomes almost atmospheric as readers' eyes move across the pages. Trauma, love, spiritualism, healing, death, violence, rejuvenation, colonization, historization, and the universe are a few of the impressions that come to mind.

Christov-Bakargiev acted, in a sense, like an insurgent—refusing to outline a straightforward concept, while placing works in many different forms of public address, not least the voluminous *100 Notes—100 Thoughts*. The series exposes the mind at work, outside the ordinary and normative bounds of academic text production. We might consider this activity of extending the exhibition into publications to be a symptom of a long retreat from the ideologies of art, as interlocutors from outside comingle with artists and curators, and books (or the internet) become an evolutionary refuge for the work. *dOCUMENTA (13)* and the methodologies it deployed to articulate exhibition willfully show changes in contemporary art and curating in which scattered and fragmented pieces are part of an intentionally (and, I would say, quite strategically and carefully) considered set of constellations. Audiences-cum-followers stitch together nodes of information and other experiential components to imagine their own narrative. Against the singularity of one identifiable thesis or predetermined conclusion, they instead can find or put together something meaningful in what they have at hand.

Christov-Bakargiev's deployment of those methodologies in such a tactical and disruptive fashion speaks to the changing modes of production that shuttle through the exhibition object. Indeed, she cracked the foundation of documenta—and, by extension, the field of curating—which rattled the scaffold holding up the institution of art's commitment to what has arguably become outmoded ideological aesthetics. "What could the word *art* be a stand-in for?" she asked. There are comparisons in her position as curator-agitator to what Susan Buck-Morss observes in Adorno when she writes, "Adorno considered that his task as a philosopher was to undermine the already tottering frame of bourgeois idealism by exposing the contradictions which riddled its categories and, following their inherent logic, push them to the point where the categories were made to self-destruct."[52]

In part, what I am working toward here is a new framework for thinking about these modes of artistic and curatorial production, and thereby imagining their mere existence as an end unto itself—where, say, research simply is, without another purpose in mind. The difficulty in picturing this proposition speaks perhaps to the extreme case of what we are getting at in this conception of postsensual aesthetics as a condition for art and the production of knowledge. Yet this extremity needs to be carefully guarded in order to prevent confining this work to the same search for truth as other disciplines, like science, in order to be perceived as legitimate. This cautionary perspective speaks to Christov-Bakargiev's resistance to acknowledging that her exhibition was a form of knowledge production. Doing so would have assigned an economic value to the cognitive labor she allied with (or against) the institution of art. Still, while there is no stated theme, and supposedly no knowledge produced, *dOCUMENTA (13)* did something in its resistance to playing to the ideologies of art and its aesthetic strongholds and protocols. It moved the dial, commanding, finally, a reassessment of the aesthetics governing art. It took into account the evolving role of curating as a form of research and imbued it with an astounding skepticism, calling into question art's capacity to meet its own unfounded, unbidden obligation to be—art. It also demonstrates that what we are examining as the curatorial is a troubling performance, or, in other words, a way to complicate things. As curator and philosopher Jean-Paul Martinon observes, the curatorial "disrupts received knowledge: what we understand by art, art history, philosophy, knowledge, cultural heritage, that is all that which constitute[s] us."[53] In this slow disintegration of the logic of the aesthetic ideologies of art, the curatorial, then, with all of its cognitive contours and lines—inside and outside the exhibition site—becomes an undeniable factor, a force, in the aesthetics equation.

Interlude

The Frankfurt School Contemporary

In his *Critique of Judgement* (1790), Kant categorizes art based on the kind of phenomenological experience a viewer has with a representation. Two modes of representation fall within the category he calls "aesthetical" art.[1] They generate two kinds of sensual experiences, each offering different levels of cognitive reflection. On what one might call the noninstrumental path, the mere sensation of pleasure that engages the subject's mental faculties causes them to interpret sights, sounds, and bodily encounters as art. Yet, in this case, the pleasure does not cause the subject to try to sort through and decipher what the art means. The sensation initiates no further motive in the subject beyond an immediate cognitive awareness of enjoyment. The instrumental path, on the other hand, occurs when a representation activates the mental faculties of the experiencing subject. The representation stimulates deeper cognitive reflection. This more intense reliance on cognition causes the subject to pause and reflect longer on the art before them.[2] This kind of encounter pushes the subject to cognitively sort out why the work is beautiful, and hence what that art communicates. What does it represent? Thus, the pleasure experienced from this mode of representation potentially has the effect of communicating something more broadly about culture or society.

Aesthetics originates from the Greek *aisthesthai* meaning "to perceive." Philosophers have long reflected on art since the time of Plato. Art's connection to a form of perception by way of aesthetics became grounded in debates based on Kant's philosophy, which has reigned over the production, distribution, and criticism of art since the Enlightenment. His ideas on aesthetics and the judgment of taste found in his three *Critiques* written in the late eighteenth century have had an extraordinary impact on what is understood, interpreted, and analyzed as art.[3] By the late nineteenth and early twentieth century, Kant's writings were dominant in academic circles and formalist programs of art criticism and historiography. They became canonized by art historians such as Heinrich Wölfflin and Erwin Panofsky, and then further instituted by modernist critics such as Clement Greenberg, who viewed the seamless unity between visual perception and representation as a key factor for determining the quality of art. The legacy of Kant's aesthetic criteria continues to resonate as a source for what the institution of art, encompassing curators, critics, artists, collectors, and academics, relies on in some capacity, whether consciously or not, to contemplate, discuss, and value art. The "aesthetic regime of art," as Rancière referred to it, comprises these philosophical frames that have long given art its internal logic. Pertinent to our study, these frameworks are what Carolyn Christov-Bakargiev would have taken into account when asking what the word "art" could be a stand-in for. They are what T. J. Demos would have considered when analyzing *dOCUMENTA (13)* in his review. They would have been on the minds of the artists, writers, and curators participating in *dOCUMENTA (13)*. In fact, they are on the minds of most people active in contemporary art today, practitioners and audiences alike. Aesthetic criteria rooted in Kant's writing, plus theories added to it over the decades, are what substantiates art's ability to distinguish itself from other parts of culture. The differentiation upheld gives art the capacity to do something that everyday objects and the phenomenological experiences of daily life cannot. Aesthetics, as we know it, therefore, ensures that art and the artist figure behave within given parameters of what have come to be understood as art and the artist figure. And while Rancière may refer to this dominance as a "regime," Adorno would call it ideology.

Adorno is a valuable reference for us. A key member of the Institute for Social Research, he was resistant to critical dogmatism and the codification of identity thinking, pursuing a critique of universality on both historical and epistemological fronts. Founded in 1923 at Goethe University Frankfurt, the Institute, commonly referred to as the Frankfurt School, operated with members and activities in various locations in Europe and the United States from the 1920s to the 1970s. Under the decades-long directorship of Max Horkheimer, the bulk of the Frankfurt School's early work in social theory sought to research and analyze the devastatingly fraught period during and immediately after World War II by investigating urgent questions related to systemically complex and narrow interpretations of historical progress. Although the early years of the Institute focused on economics and sociology, by the 1940s, key members such as Adorno, Walter Benjamin, Horkheimer, Georg Lukács, and Herbert Marcuse would concentrate on what they saw as problematic intersections of art, culture, and consumerism transpiring under the promises of the advancing technology, communication, media, and entertainment sectors of capitalism. The research not only transpired through partnerships with academic institutions; in later years, Frankfurt School members worked with government agencies, think tanks, and corporations to analyze the social and political repercussions of ideologies, such as fascism, communism, and capitalism, on society. Their work sought to propose paths toward better socioeconomic systems and new models for social reform.

As the Frankfurt School's investigations shifted from a Marxist economic critique of society to questioning the autonomy and function of art in culture and capitalism, shared assumptions about the limits of conventional philosophy to adequately analyze modern life informed new approaches to theoretical thinking. Aware of the vast and ingrained history of aesthetic and philosophical discourses onto which they were charting new theoretical territory, they chose not to graft reflections of current circumstances onto existing models that they perceived as anachronistic and irrelevant. Adorno and Horkheimer instead theorized history as a constant, shape-shifting process of becoming. History, for them, wasn't a single narrative. It was something composed of multiple strands, running parallel to one another. As early as 1931, in his inaugural lecture, "The Actuality of Philosophy," marking his entrance into the philosophy faculty of the University of Frankfurt, Adorno would boldly declare, "It would be better just to liquidate philosophy once and for all and dissolve it into particular disciplines than to come to its aid with poetic ideal which means nothing more than a poor ornamental cover for faulty thinking."[4]

So, in a move comparable to what we might categorize today as a mode of the curatorial, the Frankfurt School looked to the archival abyss of historical philosophical thinking, and selected or pulled ideas into the present to craft a contemporary school of thought that would become generally known as critical theory. Adorno and his colleagues sought to devise frameworks for analyzing the increasing instrumentalization of culture by mass media, entertainment, advertising, and technology in order to respond to the equally intensifying consumer idealism that they would eventually refer to as the "culture industry." To devise these theoretical tools, they read through philosophical thinking and made it relevant. They read through the archive, and made it contemporary.

By the 1940s, when Adorno and his colleagues of the Frankfurt School began refining their theories on art and culture, Kant's philosophy was the established criteria for the metaphysical aesthetics of art tied to transcendence. His argument for aesthetic value is an argument for the universal nature of sensation based on a subject's emotional reaction to art. But Kant's philosophy involving the individual's sensual experience would become less appealing to a mid-twentieth-century world looking to art to collectively model social change and address political problems. Adorno and his colleagues would challenge the dominance of Kant's philosophy and devise new theoretical frameworks that took into account the changing conditions of contemporary experience in order to offer thought relevant to current circumstances. They would not see art as a panacea for the problems, but they would argue for the aesthetic objectivity of art opposed to an aesthetics tied completely to the individual subject's sensual response. Adorno and Horkheimer's research would culminate in a number of published works and finally their book *Dialectic of Enlightenment* in 1947. Adorno would continue research into the aesthetics of modernist art and culture, which would evolve and transform over the years, as evidenced by an incredible number of published works, eventually informing his two signature publications, *Negative Dialectics*, published in 1966, and *Aesthetic Theory*, published in 1970, a year after his death.

Autonomy According to Adorno

Because Kant concentrates on the subject's universal experience, confusion has traditionally arisen due to his lack of clarity about the instigating source of the aesthetic encounter with art. For Kant, these originary sources against which a representation is judged are always related to the astonishing experiences one has with nature. These experiences are subjective sensory encounters, such as walking in the countryside on a sunlit afternoon and being moved by the sight of the shadows of clouds coursing across distant hills, or being destabilized by the feeling of the rush of wind against one's face from an approaching storm. These are obviously not experiences with art objects, yet these kinds of encounters with nature are what Kant measured artistic representations against.[5] For Adorno, the problems in Kant arise in the totalizing claim to universal transcendent aesthetic experience dependent entirely on the independent subject's sensual response to a representation. Adorno's critique of Kant evolves out of a broader skepticism of ingrained ideologies and universalisms, not only in art but in society, and the impact they have on how people understand history and humanity's connection to the world.[6] The rationality in Kant's critique, based entirely on a subject's capacity to reason, is determined by individual morality. This means of reasoning, which is inevitably based on personal interests and passions—and the accompanying biases—can become universal laws of judging not only art but the world and human nature. Ideology then can be instrumentalized for extreme and calculating purposes. Adorno believes there was not only one way to think about something. His critique of ideology relates to what he termed the "non-identical," a concept he conceived as antithetical to the Hegelian dialectical tradition of contradiction.

Dialectics, according to Hegel, describes the way we think and understand things and situations, shaping processes for reasoning, narrativizing history, and identifying progress and even how progress is understood. In Hegel's line of thinking, the primacy of the whole subsumes the particulars, overshadowing less traveled avenues of thought outside of the leading concept. This winner-takes-all rationale becomes enhanced by the increasing absence of nuanced perspectives because of the prevalence of dominating views. Adorno saw this approach to reason as purpose-driven, connected therefore to function, to drawing a supposedly useful conclusion. He believed that a new logic of determinism could be recovered by contradicting—in fact, by negating—these ingrained processes for how one reasons and even understands what knowledge is. He theorized that the absence of identity, or the presence of the "non-identity," as he refers to it, could help bring the particulars and fragments to the surface, disrupting the formation of grand narratives and determined perspectives. The prioritization of elements over the totality dispels ideological thinking through a kind of productive incoherence and incomprehension. Susan Buck-Morss observes, "It was this goal, the accomplishment of a liquidation of idealism from within, which Adorno had in mind when he formulated the current demands of philosophy as necessitating a 'logic of disintegration.'"[7]

For Adorno, then, the ostensibly rational thinking associated with traditional dialectics is a simplistic reduction of thought, where one thing or a concept compared to another ultimately cancels the other. This approach to developing thought, for him, could veer, as I mentioned, into ideological irrationalism like fascism, or transform into the narrativizing traditions of modernism. The line of thinking Adorno developed around the non-identical came out of his early theory of the "logic of disintegration."[8] He positioned the positivism of Hegel's dialectics into a negative, grounding his argument for what he called "the principle of non-identity." This principle would develop over the years and finally coalesce to inform his theory of "negative dialectics," which he saw as vital and necessary for reinterpreting, indeed reenvisioning, the ingrained dialectical tradition of Kant and Hegel. He would continue to refine ideas around the non-identical, which would culminate in his *Negative Dialectics*. This complex and intense study on the polemics of universalisms seeks to amplify the concept of the particular, which can offer more nuanced interpretations of things and situations, people and places, where the identification of an element over the whole negates the totalizing effect of Hegel's dialectical thinking.[9]

By applying this theory of multiplicity to the aesthetic dimensions of the art object, Adorno maintained that the subjective analysis of art beholden exclusively to the experiencing subject in Kant could be released and reassigned to the objective qualities of the object. The object, being composed of many elements, may be assessed as a composition, therefore remaining autonomous from the subjectivity of the experiencing viewer as well as from the need to provide any useful knowledge of reality. To this end, Adorno wrote,

> according to Kant, the theory of art was already potentially a theory of objects and at the same time a historical theory. The relation of subjectivity to art is not, as Kant has it, that of a form of reaction to artworks; rather, that relation is in the first place the element of art's own objectivity, through which art objects are distinguished from other things. The subject inheres in their form and content [*Gehalt*] and only secondarily, and in a radically contingent fashion, insofar as people respond to them.[10]

Adorno drew attention to the absence of clarity in Kant's writing between what art does and what it is. Kant writes a great deal about how an experiencing subject is moved by art and what art does to the subject, but less so on the originating source of that experience—a definition of "art's own objectivity." For Adorno, the art object as a thing is configured from many different factors that unite to distinguish its truth content as art, thus distinguishing it from "other things." His concept of the constellation helps to articulate this line of thought. The recognizable, individual elements can configure into a comprehensible aesthetic sign—an object or a concept. This attention to details slows down the dialectical thinking process, allowing each element to be amplified within the overall makeup of something. The elements are signifiers, electrified with meaning as they settle into a composition.[11] Adorno writes:

> The content [*Inhalt*] of a picture is not simply what it portrays but rather all the elements of color, structures, and relations it contains; the content of music is, for instance, as Schoenberg put it, the history of a theme. The object portrayed may also count as an element of content; in literature, the action or the narrated story may also count; content, however, is no less what all of this undergoes in the work, that whereby it is organized and whereby it is transformed. Form and content are not to be confused, but they should be freed from their rigid antithesis, which is insufficient to both extremes.[12]

One of the key considerations in Adorno's equation here is mediation. A work is mediated through the activation of cognitive faculties that first determine that the object is in fact art and, second, sort through what the object means. This thought process, as we can infer from above, identifies a constellation of discrete elements infinitely configurable into the totality of an art object. Adorno believed it was the responsibility of aesthetics to outline the shape of these elements so that the arrangement of nodal points would define the structure of the artwork.[13] Kant, on the other hand, made aesthetic value contingent upon the ever-shifting subjective sensual experience of the individual, surrendering any level of objectivity a representation may have to the viewer's own judgment.[14] And even though Adorno acknowledges the cognitive as part of the sensual in Kant's philosophy, he nevertheless redirects our attention away from the subjective experience to the objective qualities of the artwork without sacrificing the sensual as a crucial factor here. The mind is cognitively aware of the truth content of the art object as an aesthetically autonomous thing where whatever knowledge granted by the art is mediated by its own internal logic as art. This thought process allows the art to retain difference from the natural world. It is an art that is not affirmative of reality's daily life. The object exists. It argues for itself as art on its own terms without relying on the incontestable sensual and emotional feeling of the viewing subject or the expectation it be rational, like science, and hypothesize solutions for problems in society.

Adorno thus opened a path for considering the many factors that make up an art object. The art, although perceived in its entirety, is understood to be composed of parts. Its value is not governed by the kind of singular, universalizing theory of immanent aesthetic experience found in Kant. It is, instead, assessed by the artwork's ability to be a total thing configured from delineable elements. The elements, which include the experiencing subject, unite to communicate something. That something is grasped by the subject. Comprehension is a cognitive function occurring via a sensual, emotional experience with art. And, for Adorno, "Artistic experience accordingly demands a comprehending rather than an emotional relation to the works; the subject inheres in them and in their movement as one of their elements."[15]

What we can take from Adorno is that the contours of aesthetics can breathe and change over time; they are elastic. Art can be something else. It can be irrational and incomprehensible while still triggering cognition in the experiencing subject. By shifting the focus from a subject's universal reaction to the objective characteristics that define an art object, it is possible for an aesthetic experience with art to be something that, in line with Kant, causes the mind to reflect critically on the world. Yet, diverging from Kant, Adorno's aesthetic autonomy shows us that art is not governed solely by the subjective experience of an individual's interpretation of pleasure or emotion.[16] The artwork's elements can be parsed and analyzed individually to see how they collate into a constellation and in what ways they together leverage an aesthetic experience and claim their position as a work of art.

More recently, however, while the autonomy of a contemporary artwork is hinged to an internal logic that differentiates it from the rest of society, it is, contradictorily, imbued with a responsibility to uphold its special status as art and, simultaneously, use that status to refract everything it is not. Adorno's focus on the art object as an autonomous thing did not necessarily release it from governing ideologies. Art continues to be infused with a function of criticality while paradoxically insisting upon an autonomous position. This puts art in a bit of a double bind. And the task has proven increasingly difficult, if not impossible, in contemporary art. Art, the artist figure, and the accompanying characteristics of artistic practice, are expected to fulfill a vast range of responsibilities, not least of which, as discussed earlier, is the production of knowledge that is increasingly applicable to the ails of society.

What Role Can Art Play?

Contemporary art, undeniably, is weighted with these historical aesthetic legacies, from Kant and Adorno, combined with today's explicit reliance on art to produce meaning, to be a kind of conduit for interpreting and making sense of the world. "What role can art play?" is a question that confronts arts administrators, curators, philanthropists, educators, editors, and artists. Routinely posed by institutions and organizations, city offices, foundations, and granting agencies in meetings, mission statements, websites, and calls for applications, this straightforward query has immensely complex consequences. It presupposes that art should play a role, that it should function. And on the spectrum of functionality, the leading role it is asked to play is a critical one. All of this becomes more muddled as prominent contemporary art in the form of cultural entertainment meets the experience economy, which the field of art at present upholds economically and culturally. These circumstances are further complicated by social media, art fairs, mega-galleries, and biennials, not to mention higher education and museums. This is the industry of contemporary art. It has subsumed any autonomy that art unwittingly possessed by placing it into the service of much wider social, economic, and cultural interests of which Adorno was presciently aware, as when he stated:

> The definition of art is at every point indicated by what art once was, but it is legitimated only by what art became with regard to what it wants to, and perhaps can, become. Although art's difference from the merely empirical is to be maintained, this difference is transformed in itself qualitatively; much that was not art—cultic works, for instance—has over the course of history metamorphosed into art; and much that was once art is that no longer. Posed from on high, the question whether something such as film is or is no longer art leads nowhere. Because art is what it has become, its concept refers to what it does not contain.... It is defined by its relation to what it is not.[17]

The autonomy of art could be seen to have capitulated to consumerism or the cultural logic of late capitalism as it relates today to knowledge economies and the production of content. With art and exhibitions already solidly operating in the experience economy, we could simply accept these conditions for art as a necessary part of its evolving character. And, in fact, the more functionary position recently given to art to address pressing issues like the environment is actually a step away from the modernist ideological commitment to autonomy in which art is not expected to provide solutions to real-world problems. Maybe the fact that art holds our interest and builds a community—indeed, an entire "art world"—around it is good enough. That does not meet what Kant and Adorno describe in terms of aesthetic experience and autonomy, but it is what it is, and the present moment could be viewed as simply part of the long historical trajectory of art.

These shifting characteristics in the production and distribution of ideas and research that we have explored thus far as postsensual aesthetics signal something like this, something like a disintegration in art. The material art object is no longer the only reliable lens through which to interpret and know the world. The physical exhibition is no longer the only form of public address. The artist is no longer the singular genius figure and producer of content. These shifts are symptomatic of a transitory continuum in art and culture in which we now take part and bear witness, a period that was theorized by Hegel, to whom Adorno refers when he writes,

> Art's substance could be its transitoriness. It is thinkable, and not merely an abstract possibility, that great music—a late development—was possible only during a limited phase of humanity. The revolt of art, teleologically posited in its "attitude of objectivity" toward the historical world, has become a revolt against art; it is futile to prophesy whether art will survive it. What reactionary cultural pessimism once vociferated against cannot be suppressed by the critique of culture: that, as Hegel ruminated a hundred and fifty years ago, art may have entered the age of its demise.[18]

Christov-Bakargiev used the contemporary art exhibition as an appeal to bring together a "worldly alliance among so-called cognitive laborers of every sort, artists and scientists and fiction writers and so on."[19] This speaks to a destabilization of Kant's notion of the "arts of genius."[20] Recall that Christov-Bakargiev did not single out artists but instead identified everyone who contributed to the exhibition as "participants." She showed how the exhibition form as a thing could capture, foster, and hold work by people who do not call themselves artists. *dOCUMENTA (13)* is but one of many instances in contemporary art that demonstrate how the exhibition can act against expectations to be something else that is not completely identifiable within known parameters. Along these lines, the case for postsensual aesthetics depends on questioning the established ideals of art and the artist. Nestled in here, too, is a case for curating as a space through which practitioners may gather and move, not only to produce knowledge but ultimately to reconfigure the characteristics that define the field of contemporary art.

Adorno's theoretical methodologies were rooted in his commitment to routinely renovate established narratives and principles, including how art is judged. His interrogations into the history of philosophy exposed fissures in traditional aesthetics through which new discourses and frameworks of thought grew. These frameworks are less ideological and, therefore, applicable to evolving, contemporary circumstances in art and culture. Through Adorno, we can begin to address the impact of this lineage and potentially identify new paths that cleave the weight of historical aesthetic discourses from contemporary art. We could recognize and better analyze the breadth of ideas, research, and critical thinking by an equally broad range of practitioners from outside of art who nonetheless operate within the context of the contemporary art exhibition. The exhibition form itself, in this case, could be reenvisioned as an object with its own aesthetic values and dimensions as part of this transitory period.

Section 2

DOCUMENTA11

Curatorial Counterinsurgency

Within this developing framework for postsensual aesthetics, I want to advance our consideration of the exhibition as an aesthetic object by looking at *Documenta11*. The 2002 documenta curated by the late Okwui Enwezor was the first edition since documenta's launch in 1955 to procedurally interrogate the cultural, social, and political mechanisms and attendant aesthetic protocols of North Atlantic modernism that paradoxically brought the perennial exhibition into reality. From today's vantage point, we can see *Documenta11* as an embodiment of what Enwezor would refer to as "the postcolonial constellation," a theoretical characterization of the reformulation of thought and history reflective of the changing geopolitical landscape vis-à-vis the effects of globalism.[1] This theoretical framing of postcoloniality sees agency in contemporary art, while the exchanges in globalization offer the possibility for countermodels to the ideologies of modernist narratives. The concept parses globalism in art as a complicated organism, a constellation of nuanced and simultaneously living nodes informed by and against one another. When concept is put into practice, then, it has the capacity to amend art history, not necessarily overwriting the dominant modernist narrative, but exposing the West's narrative as one among other histories and other geographies encompassing Africa, Asia, India, the Middle East, and South America. In this regard, Enwezor thought it best to "provincialize modernism" so as to spatialize and amplify the many coexisting local modernisms.[2] This characterization of contemporary art offers new opportunities to disrupt universalisms, consequentially placing art history into what Enwezor called "a state of permanent transition."[3]

The contemporary exhibition has for decades performed as a way to write art history. With its boundless configurations of objects, situations, contexts, and ideas, then, it is also the means with which history could be undone. As Enwezor notes,

> Fundamental to the historical understanding of modern art is the important role played through the forum and medium of exhibitions in explicating the trajectory taken by artists, their supporters, critics, and the public in identifying the great shifts that have marked all encounters with modern art and advanced its claims for enlightened singularity among other cultural avatars. For contemporary art, this history is no less true, and the recent phenomenon of the curator in shaping this history has been remarkable.[4]

Documenta11 is without a doubt one such exhibition. It marks a pivotal moment when postcolonialism was theorized as a subject and actualized as a practice in the new discourses it orchestrated using experimental modes of curating.[5] From the nominating committee's selection of Enwezor, the first African, first non-European, and first nonwhite curator to be artistic director, to the curatorial team's decision to expand the traditional 100-day timeframe, and to open up the geographic scope to encompass locations outside Kassel, *Documenta11* was something completely different from earlier editions.[6] I will not rehearse here the story of *Documenta11*, for it is well known. What I want focus on is how Enwezor wielded documenta's powerful knowledge-generating capacity as part of his curatorial methodologies intent on developing discourse and thus writing art history.

At the onset, Enwezor formed a team of co-curators composed of Carlos Basualdo, Ute Meta Bauer, Susanne Ghez, Sarat Maharaj, Mark Nash, and Octavio Zaya. The collective range of their personal and professional experiences offered a kind of think tank for working with the various perspectives and regions across the globe where *Documenta11* took place.[7] More than a year in advance of the opening in Kassel, the curators initiated what they called "Platforms." Envisioned to make *Documenta11* more geographically and topically dispersed, this discursive programmatic organized activity on four continents: Africa, the Americas, Asia, and Europe. Each of the five platforms involved artists and practitioners from many countries who had never participated in documenta before and, for that matter, many contributors who did not routinely pass through the field of contemporary art.[8] With the first four platforms comprising a series of event- and talk-based activities located in or focused on parts of the world other than the North Atlantic and the fifth taking shape as an exhibition in Kassel, documenta, for the first time in its nearly fifty-year history, became conceptually and logistically global in both form and content.[9]

By 2002, when *Documenta11* opened, the biennial exhibition as an institutional form had generally matured into an arena fertile for such ambitions. It became valued for its flexibility and agility compared to a traditional museum. It was not anchored to the responsibilities and heft of a museum collection and the accompanying expectations of museum audiences. It didn't have the institutional baggage requiring it to behave like an art institution. These characteristics of the biennial's undeveloped identity, combined with its inherent contingency on place and the attendant social, political, and cultural circumstances and artistic genealogies, offered extraordinary freedom for curatorial invention. As an international exhibition of contemporary art, the biennial was uniquely equipped to address relevant, often urgent issues of the moment. Added to these conditions, the sheer number of biennial exhibitions occurring at any given time from the 1990s through the 2000s provided opportunities for emerging curators to advance new ideas and methodologies by commissioning projects, organizing programs, and publishing books.[10] It was a space for experimentation. The biennial eventually aged into a high-profile curatorial model imbued with the potential to make visible change, and to do so much faster and more expansively than by curating exhibitions or building collections for slower-moving museum programs.

As a specialist in contemporary African art, Enwezor saw the biennial exhibition as a viable platform for fashioning a global conversation around a global artistic community.[11] Before his appointment in 1998 as artistic director of *Documenta11*, he was already a respected figure in the field with a track record of using the thematic exhibition to challenge modernity's claim to universality.[12] In 2000 and 2001, he curated *The Short Century: Independence and Liberation Movements in Africa, 1945–1994* for institutions in Germany and the United States. He later remarked,

> *The Short Century* then became more than an exhibition about art as a form of cultural practice, but art as the framework through which a range of discursive activities could be articulated. My goal for the exhibition was to create not merely an event space for the reception of the radical proposals and procedures of decolonization. I wanted it to function as a concatenation of places signaling the complexity of the contemporary grammar of the postcolonial multitude.[13]

In fact, much of Enwezor's curatorial work had to that point revolved around crafting arguments on postcolonial modernity using large-scale exhibitions like *The Short Century*, as well as others such as *In/sight: African Photographers, 1940 to the Present* (1996) and *Trade Routes: History and Geography: 2nd Johannesburg Biennale* (1997).[14] Enwezor wrote that, as a curator, his "key interest has been rooted in the examination of artistic differencing through a form of curatorial counterinsurgency. I have been examining contemporary African art through exhibitions that are specifically decisive places in which the idea of the contemporary can be constituted, and, as such, are places for the creation of its meaning in relation to an enlarged global public sphere."[15]

What I'm trying to foreground is that the conditions of the large-scale exhibitions of contemporary art coalesced in the late 1990s to inform Enwezor's instrumental position as an institutional counterinsurgent and, consequently, impact how he would leverage his experience to maximize the epistemological potential of an exhibition on the scale of documenta. If the exhibition is a critical factor in writing art history, then the contemporary art curator can be seen as a primary agent for writing other art histories. Enwezor knew his influence as curator could equal or surpass that of the critic or the art historian.[16] His work as a curator made an extraordinary impact on global contemporary art because he pursued a practice committed to recovering knowledge and transforming it into discourse. Indeed, the culmination of over two decades of systemic interrogation of North Atlantic modernism initiated by Enwezor was made tangibly evident in the selection of the Jakarta-based collective ruangrupa to curate *documenta 15* in 2022, opening twenty years from the date of *Documenta11*. In a way coming full circle, the appointment of a collective not readily identifiable as either artists or curators from Southeast Asia is a spectacular demonstration that change is possible. It should not be overlooked that a member of the selection committee was Ute Meta Bauer, a co-curator of *Documenta11* and now director of Nanyang Technological University's Centre for Contemporary Art Singapore, which I discuss in Section 3.

There are parallels between Enwezor's view of the curator as a kind of counterinsurgent and Adorno's view of himself, as we examined earlier, as a philosopher undermining the institution of philosophy by working within what he perceived as an antiquated field in order to make it relevant to contemporary life. Comparisons also exist between Adorno's concept of the "logic of disintegration" and our analysis of Christov-Bakargiev's curation of *dOCUMENTA (13)*, as she radically worked within (or radically reworked) the form of documenta to make it something that did not press a singular position. In the organization of their respective editions, Enwezor and Christov-Bakargiev were both quite vocal about the importance of not telling audiences what to take from an exhibition. In his catalog essay, "The Black Box," Enwezor wrote,

> If the larger intellectual and curatorial scope of *Documenta11* is to be placed in proper perspective it is in the idea that there are no overarching conclusions to be reached, no forms of closure, and that no prognosis can be derived from the critical task it set out to examine and question, namely the idea that the means and approach taken by an exhibition is necessarily fully encrypted into the result of what it displays and the forms it recuperates for artistic posterity.... In the past, the use of the institutional forms of exhibition practice such as documenta to form a narrative, and from thence to posit a unified vision of art or to draw conclusions about its formal distinctiveness from all other kinds of practice, was central to the understanding of the institutional parameters of modern and contemporary art.[17]

The refusal to pursue one conclusive narrative consequently reflects a commitment to amplifying multiple threads that, when interwoven, suppress the perpetuation and proliferation of universalisms. In other words, a preconceived conclusion could unwittingly offer a dialectical case against, say, the modernist project, entrenching its ideology through its very negation. What I want to emphasize, though, and I believe this is in line with Enwezor's thinking, is that a critique of the modernist project is a critique of Western representation. And that critique can be waged through the knowledge associated with and produced by exhibitions vis-à-vis curatorial methodologies used to make them. Curatorial practice is a way of translating the visual organization of contemporary art into knowledge and thought, whereas the work is not necessarily about the history of art but becomes another history among others.[18]

These holistic approaches to curating signal a turn around the early 2000s where curators began to look more carefully and think more systemically about the impact of exhibition making and institution practice on knowledge production. This is important not only for our analysis of *Documenta11* but for considering the curator as an agitator—one who dispenses with predictable models of exhibition behavior in exchange for framing questions through exhibitions, and thus fashioning new narratives and ways of doing *through* the field of contemporary art. Enwezor would create an entire narrative stream by fracturing existing discourses around the very notion of the canon.[19] This was his curatorial practice. This disruption was achieved by performing documenta differently, dispersing events away from Kassel and launching activities over a year in advance of the planned opening. It was achieved by inviting a chorus of voices and perspectives by participants from fields well beyond contemporary art to contribute to the platforms and the publications. These disruptive curatorial methodologies of doing things differently actually are research on the postcolonial condition.[20]

documenta's institutional legacy was certainly a fitting context for addressing questions about the West's role in defining what is understood and valued as art, what is represented as art. As co-curator Ute Meta Bauer reminds us, documenta was "founded not just as an artistic statement but also as a political one." She saw *Documenta11* as "an opportunity to function as a corrective. For *Documenta11* in particular this can mean taking up the long overdue challenge to reformulate a history of art that is linear and focused predominantly on the West, and this in turn would necessitate that from now on we would have to address artistic positions from all parts of the world and the specific conditions under which they are produced."[21]

The *Documenta11* Complexity

The first platform, titled "Democracy Unrealized," took place in two parts over the course of spring and fall 2001 at the Akademie der bildenden Künste in Vienna and the Haus der Kulturen der Welt in Berlin. Platform 2, "Experiments in Truth: Transitional Justice and the Processes of Truth and Reconciliation," occurred in New Delhi in May 2001. Platform 3, "Créolité and Creolization," in January 2002, took the form of a workshop on the West Indian island of St. Lucía, held inside the Hyatt Regency. Platform 4, "Under Siege: Four African Cities—Freetown, Johannesburg, Kinshasa, Lagos," occurred in March 2002 at the Goethe Institute in Lagos, Nigeria. These first four platforms were organized in and around the geographic locations of interest and encompassed regional voices. The locations were also selected because of different ties participating artists and organizing curators had with them (i.e., Isaac Julien's parents were born on St. Lucía, Enwezor was born in Nigeria, Bauer served as a professor in Vienna). Eschewing an exhibition of works of art, the platforms took shape through conferences, workshops, research seminars, talks, film series, and discussions, engaging a network of practitioners, from architects, urban planners, theologists, and political theorists, to linguists, lawyers, anthropologists, and sociologists. Platform 5 returned to Kassel. It opened in June 2002 with a more straightforward exhibition of artworks by 117 artists who exhibited in documenta venues around the city.[22]

Even without knowing the names of the artists or writers who participated in *Documenta11*, or having information about where they might hail from or what their work might critique, most observers would still see that Enwezor's and his team's intervention in the time and place of documenta using the platform model signaled a different way of working with the venerable institution. To be sure, artists from other parts of the world had presented work in earlier documentas, and other curators had directed attention to activity beyond the North Atlantic.[23] But Enwezor's model was something else. The difference transpired on several overlapping layers. On its face, the most obvious focus on postcolonialism as a subject was found in art exhibited in Kassel during Platform 5. Yet any postcolonial critique that an exhibition may offer cannot be based exclusively on, say, photographs, videos, paintings, or installations about or representing the repercussions of colonialism on people and places. That's not enough for assigning *Documenta11* the significance it has today. The substantial critique posed by *Documenta11* occurs not only in the artworks, nor in one or two texts about colonialism or a written critique on the history of Westernism's long impress on its colonialist subjects. Recall that fascism, for Adorno, was the illogical conclusion of an administered society's take on enlightened reason. An ideological constraint under Enwezor's scrutiny in *Documenta11* was the ongoing phases of North Atlantic modernism enacted via the ideals of democracy and its inextricable tie to capitalism.[24] Enwezor's probing critique, then, manifested in totality in the massive and highly orchestrated constellation of activities and symposia, exhibitions and talks, and films and public programs pulled from the centrality of Kassel and integrated into other regions, including the global South. The dispersed and atomized spatial and temporal activity of the platforms pointed attention to documenta's own historical complicity in helping entrench North Atlantic modernism, so that, as Bauer wrote, "from now on we would have to address artistic positions from all parts of the world and the specific conditions under which they are produced."[25]

The *Documenta11* Books

Such interrogative critiques of Western modernity, capitalism, and democracy are, to say the least, intimidating for any exhibition to tackle. And arguably the curators of *Documenta11* did not intend to overturn the historical world order immediately with one edition of documenta. Nonetheless, more than two decades later, we see that Enwezor and *Documenta11* have changed the course of contemporary art. The complete analysis of this transformation is beyond the focus of this book. But it is within our scope to look more closely at the methodologies the curators used to explore these histories and questions, and to examine how *Documenta11* solidified its discourses for the future in the publication of eight books.[26] Bear with me here as I break down a selection of these books in the following pages in order to adequately provide common ground so that readers can have a sense of the extraordinary complexity—as a thing, an exhibition object—of *Documenta11*.

A two-volume set was published as part of the exhibition of artwork in Platform 5, which occurred in Kassel. *Documenta11_Platform5: Exhibition Catalogue* is a 620-page volume. It serves as the core book, with a collection of essays that establishes the political circumstances and conceptual underpinnings for the exhibition. The catalog has photographs of works by the participating artists and information about each of these artists. The second part of the set, *Documenta11_Platform5: Exhibition Venues*, or the so-called Picture Book, is more modest in scale yet with the same dimensions. It contains over 150 photographs of works installed at venues in Kassel. This was the first time in documenta's history that a book chronicling views of the actual exhibition was made available.[27]

Platform5: Exhibition Catalogue has essays by eleven contributors whose combined texts help situate *Docu-*

menta11 in the history of art while offering substantial reflections on a variety of topics, from postcolonialism, modernity, and urbanization, to the history of the avant-garde and cinema, to the then-recent tragedy of the September 11, 2001, terrorist attacks. Much of the writing focuses, from different points of view, on dissecting and interrogating the ideologies and realities of Western modernity. Enwezor's essay "The Black Box" lays the groundwork for the geographically atomized structure of *Documenta11* as it related to the intersection of postcolonialism and globalization, while providing an introduction to the driving concepts behind the first four platforms. Among the other essays, AbdouMaliq Simone, a sociologist and urbanist, contributed "Globalizing Urban Economies," exploring the impact of multinational corporations on urban infrastructural development and the resultant inequities between global neoliberal interests and local civic needs. Sarat Maharaj, a co-curator who is a theorist on visual art and epistemology, wrote "Xeno-epistemics: Makeshift Kit for Sounding Visual Art as Knowledge Production and the Retinal Regimes," a complex and vertiginous, even prescient, text about the technological and data-driven infrastructure controlling the movement of information and people around the globe. And Jean Fisher, an expert in the legacies of colonialism, globalization, and indigenous cultures, contributed "Toward a Metaphysics of Shit." Her essay examines the trickster figure as a necessary means toward affecting social change by undermining the institutional mechanisms that support society.

The Picture Book, *Platform5: Exhibition Venues*, published alongside the catalog, documents the representative works by participating artists Kutluğ Ataman, Luis Camnitzer, Destiny Deacon, Maria Eichhorn, Meschac Gaba, David Goldblatt, Renée Green, Candida Höfer, Feng Mengbo, Adrian Piper, Doris Salcedo, and Yinka Shonibare, among others. Enwezor, according to Bauer, remarked that he did not consider the participating artists as having been selected, but that they were making the exhibition in dialogue with the curatorial team and with one another.[28] Exhibitions and works were installed in the usual documenta venues, such as Museum Fridericianum, documenta-Halle, and the Kassel Hauptbahnhof. Plus, this edition expanded the documenta footprint by transforming a former brewery into a new exhibition site that gave *Documenta11* 65,000 square feet of additional exhibition space inside what became known as the Binding-Brauerei. The Berlin-based architectural firm Kuehn Malvezzi was responsible for the exhibition design of the entirety of *Documenta11*, including the architecture of the rooms and passages in the Binding-Brauerei. To that end, spaces were conceived and designed as highly refined, pristine exhibition galleries, comparable to those in a museum or *Kunsthalle*. The resulting impact was twofold. First, the layout forged a spatial interchange and dialogue among participating artists from a wide array of geographic locations as conjured through what was considered a series of small cities or gallery-regions. Visitors walked down a *parcours*, winding their way through the exhibition galleries in the Binding-Brauerei, many showing significant bodies of work by individual artists, whereas the walls shared by multiple artists put them visually in conversation with each other and with representative geographies.[29] Second, the exhibition aesthetic of the pristine white cube familiar to anyone who has visited a museum recreated the known institutional setting that legitimates art and narrativizes art history. Here, works by artists who had not routinely shown in such exhibition scenarios were presented alongside others, many from the North Atlantic, whose art had in fact become known through the recognizable exhibition aesthetics of the white cube gallery. *Platform5: Exhibition Venues* documents these overlaps and the conversations among places and artists, while *Platform5: Exhibition Catalogue* complements the photographic record by defining the multivalent global context and intellectual pursuits of *Documenta11*. Together, the books concretize a solid discourse on postcolonialism while demonstrating what is possible in exhibition contexts.

Although the two-volume set for Platform 5 is integral to the *Documenta11* publication project, equally substantial are the four books published to accompany Platforms 1 through 4. Platform 1 occurred in two parts, at the Akademie der bildenden Künste in Vienna from March to April 2001, and at the Haus der Kulturen der Welt in Berlin in October 2001 (just weeks after the September 11 terrorist attacks). This platform included conferences, lectures, debates, and academic seminars, many involving students and faculty from the Vienna academy. These programs combined with the essays in the accompanying book critically reflect on the unmet ideologies of democracy as advanced by the North Atlantic. Figures such as Homi Bhabha, Ernesto Laclau, Chantal Mouffe, Ruth Wodak, and Cui Zhiyuan examined the failure of democratic ideals derailed by the effects of neoliberalism and capitalism. Platform 2 occurred in New Delhi, India, with a conference and film program taking place over a two-week period in May 2001. This platform focused on the intense and urgent issues related to the justice system in India. Then, Platform 3 was a three-day workshop that took place in St. Lucía in January 2002. The workshop and accompanying publication explore how the histories, heritages, languages, and cultures of European colonialists and African slaves came to define the complex character of the Caribbean Basin, captured under the heterogeneous notion of *créolité*. With contributions by figures including Petrine Archer-Straw, Jean Bernabé, Stuart Hall, Isaac Julien, Gerardo Mosquera, Ginette Ramassamy, and Derek Walcott, Platform 3's publication has essays and transcripts of the follow-up roundtables, or "Open Sessions." In its attempts to sort out what *créolité* means today, the analyses look at cultural production, from food, urbanization, and music, to linguistics, fashion, and literature. And while that platform problematized the historic impact of colonialization on shaping *créolité*, it situated the history alongside a look at present circumstances of global capitalism, which contributes to shaping the contemporary identity of the Caribbean. Finally, Platform 4 was a conference and workshop in Lagos in March 2002, only three months before the opening of Platform 5 in Kassel. It explored issues related to urbanization and density in four African cities. These books accompanying Platforms 1 through 4 have many more commissioned texts than those mentioned here, and also reproduced other existing essays. Of the books' eighty-seven essays, seventy-two are by contributors who do not routinely participate in the field of art. Contributors came from an array of disciplines, as noted above, such as sociology, urban planning, and political science, and many of them were living and working in the geographic areas (and thus political contexts) where the exhibition events occurred.[30]

Curating Discourse

The reason I have spent some time outlining these parts of *Documenta11* in such comprehensive detail is to illustrate the truly expansive amount of ambitious programmatic activity and the breadth of voices contributing to this international exhibition of contemporary art. *Documenta11* was most certainly complex. This documenta matters as much for the artwork exhibited as for the books published and the discourse produced. It was more than a person could see in totality or easily comprehend from the individual elements at hand.[31] Yet, while the books help codify *Documenta11*'s critical position as a postcolonial project, they are part of something deeply interconnected and systemically networked in the exhibition's different forms of public address and thus its curatorial methodologies. The decision to decentralize the exhibition—conceptually, geographically, temporally—offered more visibility to other art histories, other creative, political, and cultural work than earlier editions. The amplification of this work consequently electrified other historical timeframes that, combined, characterize what Enwezor referred to as a postcolonial constellation. Nevertheless it's important to keep in mind that the greater focus on this postcolonial constellation did not attempt to negate narratives already told by the West. *Documenta11* attempted to situate new narratives alongside North Atlantic modernism, recognizing the overlapping historical strands, while, without a doubt, demonstrating the entangled, messy, and inextricable connection to Western policies, values, and institutions. Further along these lines, the critic and curator Irit Rogoff recalls, "When Okwui Enwezor was curating *Documenta11* he said again and again, in an effort to ward off the constant tedious questions about which artists were going to be included in the show, that it mattered less which artists or works he would be including than which archives he would be reading them out of."[32]

Although Enwezor may have been interested in the archive as an object of study, a prism through which to read the contemporary, he was equally interested in writing a history through it and, in turn, building an archive that would reflect, indeed refract, more granular portrayals of modernism and art history and, as such, make modernism contemporary. The *Documenta11* publications that I just reviewed were intentionally and quite strategically envisioned to accompany the platform model. Together, the books serve as a way to define, capture, and articulate the exhibition's wealth of discursive activity, geographically and temporally dispersed across the five platforms. The work exhibited in the final platform in Kassel would be read through the newly formed archival lens crafted by the first four platforms. The platform publications would become as much about producing an archive of the events and extending questions into printed matter as they would be nodes of knowledge from and through which the exhibition in Platform 5 would be read during the exhibition's time-frame and, later, into the future—today. Each platform and attendant book, while independent as things, when considered together and in dialogue with Platform 5 in Kassel, become reanimated against the larger question of global politics and contemporary art at the core of *Documenta11*.

Without a doubt, the extent to which many know and understand the exhibition today is traced to the platform books. In the conclusion to her statement quoted above, Rogoff said that Enwezor's "efforts to privilege the archives and the reading strategies at our disposal have stayed with me as an important principle of contemporaneity."[33] She is not alone. Though *Documenta11* was born from the "reading strategies" of archives, the scope and quality of criticism and documentation in the exhibition's publications carried that archive, and its corresponding mission to interrogate problematic histories and biases, into the contemporary moment. The exhibition was an epistemological space. Its curatorial methodologies and the prosthetic character of its composition of research together produced knowledge. It was a site of research that in an earlier era would be associated, at least in part, with the discipline of art history. But *Documenta11* was a contemporary art exhibition. To that end, I want to bring forward ideas introduced earlier about the precarious place that contemporary art has entered among other immaterial, knowledge-based economies and research disciplines and what this alignment means to art. Theorists such as Tom Holert, recall, cautions against positioning contemporary art with other fields of research, in turn placing more responsibility on it to continually produce and distribute information for cognitive capitalism. He writes: "The transmutation of knowledge into a sizable, measurable, and tradable entity/asset that determines the market value of individual knowledge workers (owners of expertise, experience, skills, etc.)

and entire organizations within the alleged knowledge-based economies also informs the ways in which the 'production' of knowledge in the field of contemporary art is conceived."[34]

These methodologies of artistic and curatorial research are part of the contemporary art landscape. But it's important, as Holert signals, to be aware that capitalism follows productive forms of critique—of doing things differently. It follows and makes them its own. That is capitalism's logic. While new epistemologies surface because of this work, allowing art history to be read and seen differently, the functionalized role to enhance and generate knowledge can cause contemporary art to sacrifice whatever criticality remains, precisely due to its lack of transparency and refusal to behave as expected.

Still, as discussed earlier, contemporary art, whether or not it is overtly realized by practices examined in this book, is absolutely infused with meaning-making, with making people aware of something, and thus with politics. And if the extraordinary material evidence represented by the books published for *Documenta11* are not enough to demonstrate Enwezor's rejection of the notion that art remains outside of politics, his writing attests to the production of knowledge as integral to contemporary art. One need only look at his *Documenta11* essay titled "The Black Box," where he observes that "through the continuity and circularity of the nodes of discursivity and debate, location and translation, cultural situations and their localities that are transmitted and perceived through the five platforms, *Documenta11*'s spaces are to be seen as forums of committed ethical and intellectual reflection on the possibilities of rethinking the historical procedures that are part of its contradictory heritage of grand conclusions."[35]

Contemporary art remains forever changed in the wake of *Documenta11*. Enwezor and his curatorial team's commitment to producing this discourse infused the postcolonial debate into every facet of the exhibition by using curatorial methodologies to disrupt things on a macro scale. They have encouraged every curator and every artist and every institution working responsibly in the field today to rethink and question who is saying what and who is exhibiting what and which archives the work being read through.

The Document of *Maria Eichhorn Public Limited Company*

Documenta11 created a sweeping intellectual arena to think through and expand knowledge with and among the geopolitical constituents in the platform sites. That, as stated above, was the exhibition on a macro scale. On a micro level, meaning within the exhibition itself, during Platform 5, some artists presented entire exhibitions at various venues in and around Kassel.[36] Maria Eichhorn was one of them. Upon entering the stately eighteenth-century Museum Fridericianum, Europe's first public museum, visitors could walk up the stairs and then proceed to the southeast corner. Here they found a room presenting enlarged transparencies of more than twenty pages of legal documents installed in a single row inside lightboxes, inset and mounted flush to the wall. Hung on the north side of the gallery, which is about thirty-six feet long, these works were reproductions of the founding documents of a public limited company, which included a Memorandum of Association, a Commercial Register Card, a newspaper notice, and an Agreement Concerning the Transfer of All Shares. The documents were presented in the chronological order of the corporation's life, along with a stack of one hundred 500 euro notes (the highest-value euro banknote) placed inside a steel-plated safe with a thick, transparent Plexiglas window, comparatively inset on the wall. As with the other materials, the stack of euros was displayed in chronological order, situated between a document titled "Minutes of the First Meeting of the Supervisory Board" and the "Founder's Report on the Formation of the Company." A twenty-five-foot bench was installed along the opposite wall where visitors could sit. The bench served both an aesthetic and a literal function. It was made of beech wood with dark green linoleum inlays on the seat and a modest supporting back. The bench, comparable in appearance to those used in courtrooms and government agencies, was serviceable enough as a seat to encourage visitors to linger. A wall-mounted, waist-high shelf running fifteen feet was installed on the west side of the gallery. The shelf held copies of a book of about seventy pages, with details and documents on the founding of the corporation, an introductory text by Eichhorn outlining the parameters of the corporation, and background information about the political, economic, legal, and theoretical context of the work. Visitors were welcome to read it in the exhibition space, either while standing or while sitting on the bench. They could also buy a copy at *Documenta11*'s bookshop. The text in this book, according to Eichhorn, "provides a basis from which the work can be discussed and disseminated," while establishing "the political, economic, legal and art-theory context of the work."[37] The east wall of the room was the only space in the entire museum where natural light and fresh air were allowed to enter. Here, translucent scrims were installed to conceptually connect the work to the outside world while aesthetically mimicking the illuminated light boxes.[38] This was the exhibition of the artwork *Maria Eichhorn Aktiengesellschaft*, or *Maria Eichhorn Public Limited Company*.

While these were the elements on public view, the total artwork is certainly more than what could be digested in the exhibition site. Knowledge about the processes of negotiation that made this work is also part of the artwork. To bring *Maria Eichhorn Aktiengesellschaft* into reality, the artist used 50,000 euros from the *Documenta11* budget to purchase 50,000 shares in order to launch a publicly traded company.[39] *Maria Eichhorn Aktiengesellschaft* serves as the name of this corporation and the title of the work. The Articles of Association were written at the time of the corporation's founding in March 2002.[40] The "Object of the Undertaking" in the Articles states that the "assets shall not become part of the macro-economic circulation of money and accumulation of capital or be used to create added value."[41] In other words, the assets cannot be invested, and thus they cannot accrue interest for shareholders.[42] In addition, the Articles stipulate that the corporation has a managing board and a supervisory board. The supervisory board consists of three members who are responsible for monitoring and advising the managing board, which consists of one or more members. During the first meeting of the supervisory board in 2002, Eichhorn, who is the founder, was appointed the sole member of the corporation's managing board.[43] Subsequently, she alone made the decision to transfer all shares in perpetuity to the ownership of the corporation, thereby sealing the corporation into a kind of ouroboric knot where it is owned by no one. It cannot make any decisions or changes that would allow it to earn revenue from investment. Eichhorn literalized the definition of "corporation," coming from the Latin *corporare*, that is, "combine into one body."

Under any other circumstances, *Maria Eichhorn Aktiengesellschaft* would be a conundrum. As a registered public limited company, it does not draw income because it has no way to make surplus value to generate it. It is locked into itself because the Articles of Association state that any assets obtained by way of financial contributions at its formation are to remain unchanged.[44] As a corporation, therefore, besides filing annual reports and complying with administrative and reporting responsibilities required under the Federal Republic of Germany to operate, it keeps things financially just as they are, in stasis, which runs counter to the very ethos of capitalism's continual transformation of material and immaterial labor into economic value. The work participates administratively in the capitalist system, yet it is withdrawn from the financial reasons for a corporation's existence in the capitalist system. As an artwork, *Maria Eichhorn Aktiengesellschaft* does not conceptually or even materially exist in a single representation. It is instead defined by the immaterial processes of negotiation that brought it into existence and those that continue to forge its reality. Or, as Eichhorn has stated, the work is "distinct from the material shown. It is a process or event—not an object in itself. Instead, the activities of people, set in certain time intervals constitute the work."[45] This process physically manifests in the occasionally highly managed exhibition of the parts, as described above.[46] The original records and other archival documents related to the ongoing administrative maintenance of the corporation are stored in the commercial register in Germany and are publicly accessible online. And it exists abstractly in the discourse accumulated in articles, essays, lectures, seminars, exhibitions, and talks around the ideas initiated by *Maria Eichhorn Aktiengesellschaft*.

In 2007, the Van Abbemuseum in Eindhoven made an agreement with Eichhorn to bring the work into its collection. The museum set aside 50,000 euros from its acquisition budget to repay documenta GmbH, funds which had originally been considered a loan. The transaction with the Van Abbemuseum introduced a number of complications into the stewardship and maintenance of a corporation that cannot be owned by anyone and at the same time is a work of art that refuses ownership in its intentionally corrupted form. The work, in fact, is not owned by the museum today as much as the museum is a contractual custodian. In order to exhibit it, the Van Abbemuseum has the right to present the physical components based on the written contract with the artist. The transfer of the work includes a complex legal document with words outlining the purchase of rights to exhibition and addressing other terms of maintenance—filing annual tax reports, recording meetings, paying tax and filing fees.[47] The contractually approved exhibition of the work is comparable to what was shown at *Documenta11* in addition to administrative documentation that has accumulated since that time. A second book, published as part of the Van Abbemuseum transaction, is a continuation and expansion of the version for *Documenta11*. At more than 300 pages, this book is substantially more robust, with documentation of annual maintenance records from 2002 to 2007, along with papers outlining the transfer of the work to the Van Abbemuseum. It also reproduces original documents and contains photographs of its first presentation in *Documenta11*.

The *Rose Valland Institute*, recall, which launched in 2017 at *documenta 14*, was thus not the first time Eichhorn had used an invitation to participate in a large-scale exhibition in order to inhabit the organizational structure of a public entity as an artwork. In the case of *Rose Valland*, it was as an institute; in the case of *Maria Eichhorn Aktiengesellschaft*, as a corporation. The *Rose Valland Institute* does not attempt to represent the pillaging of Jewish homes using photographs or video. Instead, the artist deploys various coordinated components (nine parts in total at its launch) and modes of public address that, together, form a discourse from the combination of activities and the exhibition.[48] *Maria Eichhorn Aktiengesellschaft*, likewise, does not represent the accumulation of capital or the ethics of monetary speculation. It does not show the challenging intersections of cultural capital in the relationships among institutions, galleries, critics, and artists. If those are the perspectives drawn from the work, they manifest instead in the pieces that come together to form the discourse around the work. The interpretation, of course, is dependent on the individual node(s) of the constellation with which one intersects. The total significance of it is not something audiences can identify from seeing a stack of bills or even from sitting inside an exhibition, no matter what stipulations are made for furniture. Any understanding or knowledge that these works offer is granted purely over time. In fact, I believe one need not even have access to the material inside the exhibition in order to "get" it. The two books published as part of the respective presentations of *Maria Eichhorn Aktiengesellschaft*—at *Documenta11* and the Van Abbemuseum—are valuable if not essential resources as far as what is needed to contextualize the work and draw together knowledge about what Eichhorn is seeking to make people aware. The books provide audiences the data and information as decidedly considered components among a constellation of exhibition forms, allowing time to sit with something and return to it later, to think about the work as a whole—in other words, to follow Maria Eichhorn.

Maria Eichhorn Aktiengesellschaft points attention to important topics that range from concepts of value, accumulation of capital, and the public accessibility of an artwork, to the ownership of knowledge production and the conditions governing artistic theory and practice. These are in fact some of the terms laid out by Eichhorn. And these are the subjects that have been addressed by writers, curators, art historians, critics, artists, and students who have studied and debated the intellectual and conceptual space of the work.[49] Yet, while these are essential takeaways from *Maria Eichhorn Aktiengesellschaft*, within our context of postsensualism—and thinking here about how contemporary art today manifests through many avenues of public address outside of exhibition—the significance for us is that Eichhorn's artworks outright refuse to grant the exhibition site the primary or only point of public contact. She has, as I stated in the Prelude, created a problem for contemporary art.[50] She is not alone. Works by all of the artists and curators we have examined thus far in the context of postsensual aesthetics complicate the expectations and function of art, exhibitions, artist, and curator. And, in turn, they trouble what are firmly understood, constituted, and interpreted forms of public address—namely, exhibition.

The Prosthesis of Exhibition and the Power of the Curatorial

Maria Eichhorn's *Aktiengesellschaft* is another kind of counterinsurgency undermining the known quantity of an entity, in this case the organizational structures of a corporation and, for that matter, an institution in the case of *Rose Valland*. She trips up the expected functionalities of artworks and exhibitions. The discourse and knowledge gained from the work does not immediately transpire in the moment of the work's reception inside an exhibition. For our purposes, I wish to emphasize that it is unleashed through a mode of production that relies on the exhibition but extends into many different public spheres, using a kind of slow-drip process of becoming. It expands the spatial and temporal character of exhibition as ideas move in and through art.

Documenta11 and many of the artworks and exhibitions in its Platform 5 presentation advanced processual forms of public address in curating, placing the onus on the immateriality of knowledge, and thereby constructing controlled and highly orchestrated epistemologies through complementary components. While methodologies differ, both editions of documenta we have examined engaged with disciplines beyond art to capture and extend the intellectual work of their participants. Knowledge production, whether utilitarian or not, is at the heart of these curatorial approaches. Returning to Christov-Bakargiev and her *dOCUMENTA (13)* statement, the curator opines, "Truthfully, I am not sure that the field of art will continue to exist in the twenty-first century. There may be some redefinitions of the fields, both in the sciences and in the human sciences, and also in between these, that may result in different ways of organizing culture and exhibitions."[51]

While it is difficult to know whether, as Christov-Bakargiev predicts, the field of art will continue to exist as this century progresses, the organization, arrangement, and rearrangement of culture and history and archives and practitioners and voices from different fields into exhibitions and publications—articulations for the public realm—will certainly go on. That work will be accomplished through curating. Her skeptical statement is a definitive nod in support of the curatorial and its "ways of organizing culture and exhibitions"—and, I would add, of making things contemporary. Instead of bringing in static objects with existing or predetermined positions and associated histories, the process of curating today has matured into a dynamic, confident, and assured space where places and things from archives and eras past point to a more clear-eyed worldview that is less singular, less determined, less static, less universal, less representative of the modernist progression of one thing after another. The power of the curatorial for defining contemporaneity is, in fact, what we learned from Enwezor and his curatorial team's organization of *Documenta11*. When reflecting on earlier editions of documenta and the history to which she was contributing, in the letter introduced at the beginning of Section 1, Christov-Bakargiev states,

> Looking at the various documenta exhibitions retrospectively suggests that there has been a shift from a diachronic movement of art to a synchronic movement of curatorial practice, from the experimental avant-garde's historical self-positioning in a forward movement (from one generation to the next, from one art movement or concept of art to the next) to a practice that detemporalizes art into a geographic and spatial expansion of the field (bringing artists from different parts of the world together, acting in between

> geographies), which has gone hand in hand with an increase in projects related to struggles and causes around the world.[52]

The inherent choreographic character of the curatorial offers a kind of disc jockey modality, orchestrating a symphony of individual pieces and parts, voices and time periods, playing and moving—dancing—in the space of contemporaneity. The curatorial not only moves in synchronicity with these changes in art but has become the locus of instituting them.

The curation of *dOCUMENTA (13)* and the decade or more of large-scale exhibitions and changes in academic programs (undoubtedly influenced by *Documenta11*) are symptomatic of a forward trajectory in which the practice of curating is necessary for activating the diachronic character of art. These exhibitions demonstrate a mode of curating that reveals how contemporary art can be something else.[53] When exhibition becomes less coherent as a thing, less constricted by a predetermined theme or thesis, less recognizable, then the form becomes fertile ground for instituting change with its own indecipherable behavior.[54] Those were the possibilities initially offered by the biennial form before it, too, codified into institution. Meanwhile, under these conditions, curatorial approaches operate as philosophical modes, forming the basis for the curatorial, and its attendant mode of production—the exhibition—to function as a kind of prosthesis.

To that end, the curatorial, as a concept and mode of production, shapes these kinds of elements into a proposition. In this light, the exhibition can be considered an object with multifold, prismatic qualities possessing an aesthetic dimension that a contemporary theoretical framework like postsensualism can take into account to make anything contemporary. Returning again to Rogoff, the critic-curator writes, "Not only is contemporaneity about the engagement with the urgent issues of the moment we are living out, but more importantly it is the moment in which we make those issues *our own*. That is the process by which we enter the contemporary."[55]

As an aesthetic form, the exhibition, when realized with the curatorial methodologies examined thus far, operates in step with contemporary life. The curatorial continuously retools everything—including the archive—so that ideologies rooted in canons of art history or biases in sociopolitical legacies of modernism can be challenged. Without the curatorial, something—concept, history, archive, place—can be left hanging in space without context, moving boundlessly without relation to anything else.[56] The curatorial, then, brings these elements into dialogue with time and place. Enwezor's description of the curatorial counterinsurgency, as well as the statements by Christov-Bakargiev cited above, expose a decided skepticism about art's continued existence, at least in its current aesthetic form. Their contributions are part of a larger chorus in theory and in practice signifying that something's up, or is faltering, in art—and suggesting, in turn, the need to take a clear-eyed accounting of the qualities of exhibition as critical factors in any aesthetic framework. The exhibition acts as a prosthesis in this vein. It holds up the art object, in some cases to the ideological constructs against which the very curatorial methodologies react. The contours of the prosthesis are identifiable in other disciplines increasingly taking part in contemporary art, with the physical exhibition increasingly extending into other kinds of public address. The artists and curators whose work we have examined have identified how to interpret, reflect, change, and communicate ideas that are read in and through the field of art. They understand how to inhabit the form of fragmentation. And, today, they no longer rely on the art object, or even the known parameters of exhibition, to do it all.

Section 3

CENTRE FOR CONTEMPORARY ART SINGAPORE

Knowledge Economies

On February 28, 2021, Nanyang Technological University's Centre for Contemporary Art Singapore closed its exhibition hall and concluded its regular public programming at Gillman Barracks.[1] The former British military complex had served as the primary site for NTU CCA's exhibitions, public programs, residencies, offices, and research since the Centre's opening by Ute Meta Bauer in 2013.[2] NTU CCA was the anchor organization in the sprawling precinct, which is home to several international galleries as well as restaurants and bars. Gillman Barracks is an economic redevelopment project envisioned to radically transform the military grounds, originally built around 1936, into a center for arts and culture in Singapore. NTU CCA's presence drew thousands of visitors annually, advancing the economy in the region while providing wider visibility for the arts scene in Southeast Asia. By many accounts, the seemingly unconventional partnership between a university and a city's economic development board to open a cultural institution dedicated to the contemporary arts and research among commercial entities was a success.[3] Nevertheless, the expiration of a start-up grant provided by the Singapore Economic Development Board, combined with the absence of financial commitment from the university, caused NTU CCA to cease operation of its public-facing programs at Gillman Barracks.

I want to focus our attention on Bauer's work at NTU CCA Singapore for a few reasons. The Centre's institutional infrastructure was envisioned to foster a wide range of artistic and curatorial production by placing work alongside and integrating it into a research university. Also, Bauer's curatorial methodologies at NTU CCA rehearsed how an arts institution could enact different curatorial propositions to serve audiences, artists, and curators while tending to competing economic interests. Furthermore, reflecting on the curatorial work at NTU CCA allows us to look further into the systemic traces of *Documenta11*, not only its impact on the appearance and shape of short-term presentations of artistic and curatorial production, as we examined in Christov-Bakargiev's *dOCUMENTA (13)*, but also its influence on long-term institutional practice and artistic research.

NTU CCA is academically part of a university with undergraduate and graduate departments spanning science, engineering, and medicine, as well as humanities departments administered by the university's College of Humanities, Arts, and Social Sciences. With its high-profile place as a research center for the contemporary arts in Singapore, the Centre quickly became part of a larger institutional scene in Southeast Asia, a region with its own complex history of arts, education, and economics. The art historian T. K. Sabapathy has for more than four decades reflected on this history in his writing about modern and contemporary art and the development and changes in work by artists and curators in Southeast Asia.[4] His criticism, teaching, and advising have made his work an essential record of the evolving landscape of contemporary art and education. While there is much to be gained by looking at Sabapathy's vast body of writing, his accounts of arts education in Singapore are useful for our purposes.

In fact, the expectation for education to have a functional role in Singapore dates to the years following Britain's colonialization in 1819. Britain's education policy was designed to prepare Singaporeans to work in government and commercial agencies. The study of English language, history, and literature, for example, and proficiency in mathematics and legal systems were aimed at inspiring loyalty to the British Empire while practically supporting needs for an efficient workforce that could protect Britain's economic and political interests. Art and arts education were not a priority in this scheme.[5] Even after independence in 1965, the study and practice of art was not accorded high priority in the formation of the new state. The perception inculcated a belief, which continues to resonate, that art is valuable when discernibly tied to economic interests. The gravity of this history is reflected by the noticeable absence, until relatively recently, of a critical mass of museums and art academies.[6]

Focusing on research and knowledge production, however, is one way art institutions in Singapore have been able to substantiate and argue for their value. In the years after independence, research in the arts was primarily associated with writing, specifically as it relates to the discipline of art history. Sabapathy's own work represents a commitment to narrativizing a history of modern and contemporary art. Knowledge gained by studying art history is useful, and is drawn from an academic discipline whose parameters are known. A published text, in other words, is a source of information and data that becomes applicable to learning about social, economic, and political situations and regions. In more recent years, the increasing expectation that contemporary art can stimulate the economy through tourism with festivals such as the Singapore Biennale (launched in 2006) has become a stronger and more viable argument for the arts. In addition to its perceived impact on economic and urban development, contemporary art, as discussed earlier, has superseded the place of learning once held exclusively by the domain of art history, further reinforcing expectations that contemporary art can instigate change by offering solutions to real-world problems. Higher education in the arts is complicit in this long transition. Tom Holert's perspective on the epistemological turn in contemporary art is applicable to these circumstances:

> Artistic practice in a neoliberal research university is now being integrated, if at different speeds and with local variations, in a steadily globalized, transnational domain of higher education in the arts. Here, notions such as "artistic research" or "art-based research" have proved instrumental in associating contemporary art with a mode of knowledge production that is adapted to and managed by the very institutional facilities that previously gained their authority by disempowering the critical agendas of the humanities and social sciences. What used to be a practice of challenging epistemic norms—for instance, process-oriented and post-object art—has become an integral part of contemporary knowledge economies.[7]

Questions around the urgency for institutions to foreground art's epistemological value as it relates to "knowledge economies" describe the institutional arena in Southeast Asia and at Nanyang Technological University into which NTU CCA entered in 2013. The Centre was not, however, the only educational department in the arts at NTU. Founded in 2005, the School of Art, Design, and Media (ADM) at NTU, where Bauer also serves as professor, offers a curriculum in graphic design, animation, cinematography, digital communication and website development, and advertising. The school is committed to graduating students who can participate in the creative and technology industries. Teaching and learning in NTU ADM are often administered with identifiable learning outcomes valued for their connection to commercial sectors. NTU CCA's founding marked the beginning of something different. It was the first time NTU had introduced art as a field of research in and of itself without a definitive, applicable end to something tangible. The goal was to integrate into the academic ecosystem artistic and curatorial research methodologies without prescribed outcomes. This mission was tricky. It proposed to elevate research as a mode of autonomous critical inquiry without adhering to the same protocols of, say, proving a mathematical formula in engineering or testing a hypothesis in the natural sciences, while simultaneously working in a university setting where the value of research and education are measured against viable application. NTU CCA nevertheless proceeded with its mission by using what was referred to as a "three-fold constellation" of institution practice. The first three years of programming were organized around the broad concepts "place," "labor," and "capital" with programs both public and private taking place through residencies, research, academic education, and exhibitions.[8] Then the MA in Museum Studies and Curatorial Practices launched in 2018; although co-administered by CCA and ADM, the program is self-sustaining. Graduate students work with Bauer, university faculty, and visiting research fellows. The program also employs part-time faculty who are practicing artists or creative professionals in the field—specifically in Singapore for many years—and are invited to teach.[9]

NTU CCA's organizing framework and its attention to cultivating networks in Southeast Asia fostered a substantial discourse on the arts and a focus on the region in a relatively short period. This was accomplished through a methodology that Bauer and her team call the "Spaces of the Curatorial." The curatorial, as we have explored, describes bringing together different points of reference—ideas, concepts, objects, materials, histories, constituents—into physical and conceptual arenas where they become relevant to one another and to the circumstances of time, place, and people. To that end, NTU CCA invited artists, curators, and writers to Singapore as part of its residencies program. The visiting practitioners intersected formally (and informally at their own discretion) with networks in Southeast Asia. Related to this work at NTU CCA and the totalizing approach to curatorial practice we have been considering, Bauer writes,

> The curatorial emerges out of an interplay of connections and layers that are often set up in opposition to or in unexpected relations. This process gives shape to a specific space for the public to encounter, experience, and engage critically with forms of cultural production that bear a sense of the urgency of the now and have relevance in the wider social sphere. Such a "space" can be an exhibition, a publication, or a talk, while the process of making this happen and manifestation from production to communication carries the trace of curatorial thinking in such a way that they all contribute to the overall mode of addressing the public. The approach towards curating as a complex, multilayered mode of production accounts for NTU CCA Singapore's vision of a holistic institution defined by the reciprocity and entanglement between exhibitions, residencies, and research and education.[10]

The Institution Object

Before proceeding, recall that we have advanced the framework for postsensual aesthetics by identifying and analyzing the multifaceted visual and cognitive characteristics of the art object in work by artists Amy Balkin, Maria Eichhorn, and Claire Pentecost, and in the exhibition form or object in work by curators Carolyn Christov-Bakargiev and Okwui Enwezor. Now, we can apply comparable analysis to what I call the "institution object" in the holistic institution curated by Bauer at NTU CCA. In each case, the characteristics associated with the curatorial are seen as pulling together and articulating various elements that combine to compose the aesthetic dimensions of the object—be it artwork, exhibition, or institution.

When considering NTU CCA as an institution object, then, it can be viewed as having two distinct yet conceptually related concentric rings of activity rotating at different paces. The *interior ring* moves at the pace of research-based work undertaken by the invited artists, writers, and curators. These practitioners came into and moved through the institution contextualized by one or more elements of the threefold constellation model—

exhibitions, residencies, and research. Sometimes they did not have a public presence at all. Invitations were extended with the expectation that artists were interested in pursuing research related in some capacity to topics like place, labor, and capital, or, in later years, climates, habitats, and environments.[11] The mere presence of visiting practitioners at the Centre, as I have suggested earlier, placed them in dialogue with the greater interdisciplinary offerings of the university, not to mention larger networks in Southeast Asia.

Farther out from the center of activity, the overarching concept determined by the institution could be considered an *exterior ring* (or rings) composed of several general topics cycling through the institution more slowly, more methodically, at any given moment. Each exterior ring could hold the various components drawn from the interior that become activated when considered against each other and in relation to time and place. The invited practitioners possess ideas on the topics the Centre decides to foreground, and the knowledge they produce is marshaled at the will of the institution. The individual sources of knowledge then contribute to a larger, integrative discourse articulated and framed by the institution, yet not instrumentalized from the onset for that purpose. The research is there. It exists—kind of like an archive. It becomes relevant through the curatorial.

As imagined above, then, the organizational structure of NTU CCA echoes the ways in which the platform model functioned for *Documenta11*. While each platform was an autonomous node, when it was considered alongside other platforms and within the greater context of the *Documenta11* project, each practitioner can be said to have contributed to the overall discourse produced by that edition of documenta. Yet that discourse was framed by the institution, so the knowledge positioned within that context became activated. Along these same lines, NTU CCA shows how the temporary exhibition-making modalities of a large-scale exhibition like documenta, Manifesta, or the Venice Biennale can become institutionalized. Within our context, it reveals how the characteristics of postsensual aesthetics can extend to describe the institution as a thing—as an object. At the level of the individual practitioner, taking Maria Eichhorn as an example, the different nodes of work—an exhibition of household goods and books owned by a deported and executed Jewish family, a workshop about the dissolution of private property during the Nazi regime, a call for papers on unlawful ownership in Germany, and the launch of a research institute dedicated to studying the history of looted objects—are all brought together to form an art object that furthers a discourse, in Eichhorn's case about dispossessed property during the Nazi era. At the level of the institution, in the case of NTU CCA, we find that it coordinates comparable nodes of knowledge in the form of cultural production in order to build a discourse. This discourse can range and rove widely, from the role, function, and precarious pitfalls of a contemporary arts institution as an economic urban redevelopment tool in Southeast Asia, to directing more attention to the activity of small-scale arts institutions scattered throughout the region. The multidimensional character of these combined factors—the "Spaces of the Curatorial"—helps define the discourse.[12] As a theory and a practice, it mobilizes and choreographs knowledge produced by practitioners, who themselves intersect with a constellation network comprising what I am calling the interior ring. Their work adds something else, dependent on how the research is framed and applied (or not) by the Centre, without necessarily serving to illustrate a thesis or theme.

At NTU CCA, these curatorial methodologies became a performative institutional critique of a neoliberal university's systemically fixed boundaries on artistic and curatorial production combined with a reminder of the ongoing negotiations institutions have with funding structures. Bauer is certainly familiar with navigating the intersections of art, economics, and urban development. In her thirty-year career as a curator, administrator, and educator, she has worked with organizations where the life of an institution or a biennial was deeply interwoven into the wellbeing of a region's urban and economic health. Indeed, shortly after serving as co-curator of *Documenta11*, she was named founding director of the Office for Contemporary Art Norway in Oslo in 2003. OCA is an institution that supports the contemporary arts throughout Norway, collaborating with international partners on exhibitions, publications, and residencies.[13] During her tenure, Bauer became a leading voice in New Institutionalism, a term used to describe curatorial and administrative methodologies that rehearse different behavioral and economic models for contemporary arts institutions.[14] The praxis-as-research approach embraces experimental funding structures and innovative curatorial platforms. While less common in parlance today, in the early 2000s, New Institutionalism initiated a substantial discourse around the precarious intersections of private interests and public administration. And, comparable to the circumstances that NTU CCA faced with Gillman Barracks, these approaches to "curating the institution" involve exploring different avenues for arts initiatives co-funded by the state and private sources, which, at times, can put the institution at the mercy of the economic and cultural capital they are relied upon to generate.

Bauer and her team organized a project that I will use as a concrete work to illustrate how these concepts related to the curatorial were manifested in reality. My intention is to demonstrate how the framework we have developed for postsensual aesthetics is applicable for analyzing NTU CCA.

The Making of an Institution

The Making of an Institution was curated by Bauer with Anna Lovecchio, the Centre's curator of residencies, and Anca Rujoiu, curator and manager of publications. Occurring from February 11 to May 7, 2017, it was an expansive project composed of three parts: an exhibition, a series of public programs, and a publication. It opened over three years after NTU CCA was founded and served as a self-reflexive accounting and evaluation of the institution's work to date, a cataloging of its history—in the making, one could say—while positing what the future could hold. Working with artists, curators, writers, and designers from Singapore and beyond, the project reflected on what an institution could and should be. It foregrounded questions about how an institution could demonstrate its commitment to audiences, as well as cultivating and building a network. It explored questions about how to serve a research community like Nanyang Technological University while meeting the expectations for an urban redevelopment project like Gillman Barracks. *The Making of an Institution* was comparable to a public report.[15]

In the galleries at Gillman Barracks, works by a selection of artists- and curators-in-residence were shown. Some of the work was not artwork at all, although called to the public realm to represent the behind-the-scenes cognitive research and ephemeral social assembly that contemporary art institutions like NTU CCA support. Much of the material could have been considered an archive—or maybe a core sample—of ongoing research temporarily arrested in order to surface publicly in the exhibition. The demand to physically materialize on the occasion of an exhibition is part of what we have examined with the framework of postsensualism. Artists and curators devise ways to utilize the exhibition form to introduce a body of work that often requires the presentation of documents, archives, and other materials to make visible what is actually immaterial labor. Audiences then reciprocate by giving time and attention to read what is presented in the exhibition, even though it does not represent the entire work and may not even be artwork. Yet reading, either on site or beyond the exhibition's physical or temporal frame, helps reveal the complexity of a larger project, the totality of which is simply unrecoverable in one exhibition experience.

That was the case for the Singaporean artist and writer Heman Chong. He used his residency to launch a project called *The Library of Unread Books*, organized in collaboration with the archivist Renée Staal. Hosted in Chong's Gillman Barracks studio and open on Fridays during the run of the exhibition, the project invited visitors to become library members by donating one unread volume.[16] Quickly accruing a collection of over 300 books from the beginning of Chong's residency in September 2016 to the opening of the exhibition in February 2017, the project explored what the visual mass of unwanted immaterial knowledge looks like. While the notion "unread" has connotations of being "unwanted," the physicality of books piled on tables signified something else: it made materially visible the human aspiration to produce knowledge. The by-product consequentially became an informally drawn portrait of human aspirations to consume knowledge. In other words, at some point in the life of each book, the title caught the attention of its previous owner and seemed capable of fulfilling their yearning to know more and their optimism that they could better understand something, whether becoming versed in writing by James Joyce or skilled in effective social media tactics.[17]

When Chong's project was presented in the exhibition hall, piles of books stacked on tables represented the work. The presentation of books was punctuated with props made by the American artist Joan Jonas, which were part of her earlier exhibitions and residencies at NTU CCA. The props, which had remained in Singapore in storage after Jonas's projects closed, could be interpreted as archival objects in themselves. They were reanimated when placed in relation to Chong's library inside the gallery. Chong's painting *A History of Amnesia* (2016) from his ongoing series since 2006 of paintings of speculative, self-designed book covers of actual titles (all acrylic and all the same size, 18 x 24 inches) accompanied the presentation of *The Library of Unread Books.* He also contributed a text titled "The Book of Drafts (Part 2)" to the publication accompanying *The Making of an Institution.*[18]

The public programs component of *The Making of an Institution* included a series of informal talks related to the Centre's residencies organized under the title *Artistic Research*. These talks occurred mostly in the exhibition hall. Another series of formal lectures called *Reasons to Exist: The Director's Review* took place in the screening room. Directors, chief curators, and founders of institutions from London, Utrecht, and Singapore to Yogyakarta and Dhaka reflected on their motives for managing and leading their institutions and the connection each has with regional contexts.[19] Participating speakers shared similar commitments to artistic research as part of wider global conversations in contemporary art while also seeking to be in dialogue with their respective localities. In another series of lectures, organized under the title *Communication and Mediation*, graphic designers and architects talked about the roles of visual and spatial identity in the ways institutions address their publics and build audiences through different, often parallel, streams of online, visual, and wayfinding communication.[20]

The third component of *The Making of an Institution* is a 444-page book titled *Place.Labour.Capital*, released a year later, in 2018, by Mousse Publishing. This capstone, however, is more than a straightforward manifestation of the exhibition. *Place.Labour.Capital* serves as a broader reflection on the endeavors, activities, and challenges of the Centre in its first three years of existence—something in between the archival and the institution-autobiographical. The book is packed with an extraordinary wealth of documentation: photography of exhibitions, programs, and residencies, an archive presented alongside new and existing texts by more than eighty contributors. While a complete record of the institution's activity during that timeframe, the accompanying written criticism parsed questions related to the intersections of cultural production, economics, and artistic research. The combined content, exceptional in intellectual depth and archival detail, positions NTU CCA's pursuit of knowledge production through artistic research as part of the methodologies associated with the curatorial, as well as within wider social, political, and economic circumstances in Southeast Asia.[21]

Learning to Unlearn

Among the written contributions in *Place.Labour.Capital* is an essay titled "The Human Factor" by T. K. Sabapathy. It is the very first text in the book and was commissioned for the publication. Sabapathy attempts to situate NTU CCA's commitment to artistic research within the complicated historical trajectories of arts education and artistic research in Singapore. He argues that disciplines must have identifiable methodologies for research, that the parameters of artistic research should be known and visible—like the research methods used in art history. Sabapathy finds the absence of protocols for artistic research at NTU CCA problematic. In the case of the curator residencies, the invitation, recall, had nothing overtly to do with contributing to the larger NTU CCA program other than to place curators in dialogue with the university and the greater Singaporean and Southeast

Asian communities. Visiting curators were not required to leave anything. This kind of invitation, for Sabapathy, meant that nothing was at stake for the visitor or the institution. The informal connections to the regional scene without leaving material proof was not enough. He argued,

> I know that one of the strengths of a residency at NTU CCA Singapore is the non-demand that you should leave something tangible. I have no problems with that; I support such a provision. But as a research institution, I don't think we can just stop there. There have to be ways of making marks and collecting traces, otherwise knowledge is impossible. Knowledge is relational, it is cumulative. Yesterday's experience and work is the basis for today's knowledge. Today's knowledge is the base of tomorrow's and so on. And if this is not there, then there's nothing.[22]

The deep-rooted ideologies associated with education in Singapore—indeed, the expectation that artistic research "should leave something tangible"—continue to linger, even for the informed. It is noteworthy that Sabapathy's essay is placed in the first pages of *Place.Labour.Captial*. This prominent position at the onset of the book foreshadows the argument for artistic research that the book posits. Contrary to what he writes, there are, in fact, significant traces of this research at NTU CCA. The traces, however, do not look the same as those left by art history or other fields of knowledge production, like science, medicine, or engineering.

Bauer and her team meticulously documented the institution's work and archived it in *Place.Labour.Captial*. Not unlike *Documenta11*'s attention to recording and archiving its wealth of discourse in the platform publications, NTU CCA produced a remarkable number of archival media, from photography and video to exhibition guides and installation shots, to videos of lectures and PDFs of entire books. Most are accessible from the Centre's digital archive, which was launched in March 2021 shortly after the public closure of the exhibition hall, in part to assure that the Centre's work and research would remain publicly visible—and in some ways more accessible than it had been previously. The online content and the book stand as the primary sources for critical reflection about the institution. These archives become institution practice made visible. Many of the figures whose exhibitions we have examined look to the archive as both the work and the product of work. Earlier, I mentioned that Maria Eichhorn's *Maria Eichhorn Aktiengesellschaft* was an ouroboric knot sealed unto itself. The work is the ongoing research *and* the manifestation of research. The actual labor is cognitive, a performance captured by "something tangible," like what is shown in spaces where it is made public. This capture, whether it takes the form of exhibition, publication, or website (or a combination thereof), is strategically conceived as necessary. The ephemeral and time-based nature of cognitive labor and social assembly needs to materialize in the public realm. Yet what is offered in the public realm cannot be absorbed in a singular form of presentation like an exhibition; the object historically required is elusive. Thus, the drive arises to produce books as part of the work. Herein lies the crux and the urgency to consider the crucial role that cognition plays in the overall aesthetic dimensions of these kinds of research- and archival-based works—whether artwork, exhibition, or institution—and with it, the framework that postsensual aesthetics can offer.

The curator and writer Chus Martínez suggests the need for a kind of unlearning of the syntax of research, not necessarily to erase existing epistemologies, but to consider new ways of knowing that do not mean gathering information in order to ground it in a body of knowledge. She writes:

> This vacillation—caused by the artistic method of conveying research into the real, into an artwork—has the virtue of perceiving the unknown without its being transmitted into communication by the superficial sociality of the discourse. To refract the unknown without syntaxes, without the movement of displacing the known and replacing it with a new known or

> the other known: this momentary forgetting of the syntaxes implies a momentary forgetting about learning—that is, it can carry the unknown into a form, a formulation, that will allow the inconceivable to be conceived.[23]

Martínez advocates for reconditioning what is understood as research. In this case, processes involving the recovery of information could be seen as methodologies, whereas the production of knowledge in and of itself is the procedural act of assembling voices in space (whether it is physical, print, or digital space). NTU CCA's "Spaces of the Curatorial," or the curatorial assembly, however one chooses to phrase it, then, becomes a momentary capture of elements suspended and read against ever-evolving constellations of time, place, and context.

Exact Imagination

Audiences of contemporary art increasingly encounter an aesthetic form that, by design, demands further reading and attention—and this is because the components, whether artwork, exhibition, or book, are like core samples extracted from much larger and conceptually entangled bodies of work. In these circumstances, it is in fact impossible to experience the totality of the thing they are encountering in that moment. Presentations of work like this are often a cross-section of the ongoing research that has been iterated in previous exhibitions and books, and may return in others yet to come. Whether an artwork by Maria Eichhorn or an exhibition by Carolyn Christov-Bakargiev, the modes of production used in these practices involve sophisticated curatorial methodologies. The artists and curators whose work we have examined all think curatorially, taking into account how individual elements configure into an overall aesthetic form. They take advantage of the facts that the work cannot be experienced at any one time, in any one place, and that cognition is an essential factor in audiences' aesthetic engagement with it.

A thread connecting the work discussed in this book is the willingness of audiences to meet these atomized characteristics—to "follow"—by organically and spontaneously performing a kind of cognitive bridge-building, piecing together various parts of a work to arrive at meaning. How do we analyze this activity as a mode of curatorial production, and in what capacity does it correspond to the theoretical framework of postsensual aesthetics? In this final section, I look to Adorno's concept of "exact imagination," which embodies and interweaves his criticism on ideology and the idea of the constellation that we have appropriated and traced in earlier pages.[1]

Adorno theorizes exact imagination as something that transpires in the experiencing subject through the combined factors of knowledge, lived experience, and aesthetic form.[2] Exact imagination acts as a kind of catalyst among consciousness and the bodily experience of being human, in which the subject—viewer, listener, reader—of a work of art undergoes a quasi-logical and quasi-sensual encounter with an object. Subjects apply the combination of knowledge and experience to electrify imagination; imagination in turn reads and configures signifiers into an aesthetic experience of the object. The thought process should theoretically allow one to bridge the divide between ideas and one's physical and cognitive experiences of art to draw out an individual interpretation of something that does not permanently gather into a totality. It remains, in other words, "constellated." Exact imagination slows down and atomizes aesthetic engagement with the object, wherein the audience is able to decipher and follow its internal logic in a mimetic process of imagining the contours of the aesthetic form, which is not completely present before them.

To that end, the experiencing subject today accepts that a certain amount of continued cognitive engagement is necessary over time and beyond the initial spatial encounter of a work of art or an exhibition. Contemporary audiences have acquired the capacity to produce a level of knowledge about a work by reconfiguring the material and immaterial parts at their disposal. They use a combination of cognitive awareness and the quasi-sensuousness achieved through a learned understanding of how to parse, or even mime, the experience of a work. Through this mimetic or rote sensuousness, gathered by reading something in a book or seeing something in an exhibition, they have a "performative" aesthetic experience. They understand that what they have before them is partial, in many respects. They have before them the idea. They synthesize, in this case, the "truth content" of an art object, which Adorno regarded so highly as part of analyzing the autonomy of art, composed as it were from a constellation of components. His theory can be applied to analyzing the aesthetic dimensions of the exhibition object. The exhibition object reaches across time and place, from the presentation of materials within the space of an exhibition to the reading of texts in a publication at home. All the same, the factors are connected; they interweave to form the object. And, although the sensuality of a physical encounter is missing in the actual moment of aesthetic engagement with a book, for example, the subject nevertheless has a cognitive response.

Aesthetic experiences constructed from what Adorno calls exact imagination, whether in the space of the gallery, in a seminar at an academy, through the pages of printed media, or through the illuminated pixels of the screen, are each an opportunity to enter a work at different literal and conceptual moments. Much of what we know and digest about art is not based on physical contact with the object or the space of exhibition. It is, in fact, conceivable that through the combined factors of lived experience, knowledge, and the recognizable form, an aesthetic experience is possible even without having an actual encounter with art because the idea or concept is familiar, and it is present in the audience's mind.

This final point could be seen as the very crux of the problem for art and shows why reconsidering the aesthetic frameworks for contemporary circumstances is necessary. In other words, while exact imagination might be a way to mitigate the dissonance among the fractured pieces of a work of art, it exposes fault lines in art when considering what Adorno calls "late work" or "late style."[3] In the mimetic process inherent to his theory of exact imagination, he describes how the subject draws on previous encounters with works of art: they enter an engagement with artwork already loaded with knowledge and experience on how to interpret something. If a work of art has an interpretable style, the subject can quickly assign it to a category; it can be recognized as something by a specific artist; it can be associated with a period; its political position can be quickly deduced. The experiencing subject is equipped with cognitive tools to construe meaning through the ready interpretation of that style—the appearance. The contemporary subject is then willing and able to accept the effect of ingrained ideologies of art. This willingness to simulate an aesthetic experience draws on the long historical trajectory of the subjective in art. This subjectivity, though, has the capacity to liquidate art through the repetitive tracing and retracing of encounters between the experiencing subject and the objectivity of the artwork, repeated until it has become conditioned over time.

Regarding this point, Adorno observes,

> The contents which interpretation tries to grasp have changed completely in reality and thereby in the works as well, which stand within history and participate in real history. History has uncovered and made evident the original contents within the works; they are visible solely by virtue of the disintegration of their gestalt-like unity in the form of the work, and it was only the closed unity of the two that provided the space for adequate interpretation. Today interpretation wanders around lost among the fragments. It can recognize the contents, to be sure, but it cannot draw them back into the material from which history has dislodged them.[4]

If we follow Adorno's argument, there is no longer any such thing as a work of art outside of the history of mimetic nature. As experiencing subjects, we have systemically developed over time an astute capacity for recognizing and responding accordingly to an art object. In other words, perhaps the historical progression of the history of art and all of its aesthetic traditions and knowledges has reduced the art object and even stripped it of its capacity to be art. A subject's experience over time does, without a doubt, refine and almost perfect the analytic tools to imitate a response to an aesthetic form whose qualities are recognizable as art. We see it as an idea. This is something we cannot deny.

Within our context, Adorno's exact imagination, on the one hand, gives a theoretical framework for interpreting modes of production that use curatorial methodologies to produce and disseminate work that ultimately relies on cognition to engage subjects. On the other hand, exact imagination exposes the dissonance today between the ideologies of art and the realities of the art object. This dissonance encourages us to look more generously at the exhibition as object. While Adorno's exact imagination may no longer be as applicable or relevant to the objectivity of the art object, we could look at the exhibition's contextual framework, ever shifting and changing in synchronicity to the moment, as a way to recover the aesthetic dimensions and resuscitate the life of the aesthetic form—the diachronic character of the art object—in the contemporary moment. In this case, all objects have the capacity to enter contemporaneity. They can be framed within the logic of curatorial methodologies by recasting Adorno's exact imagination onto the exhibition object. According to this logic, the theoretical frame of postsensual aesthetics is inherently tied to a knowing awareness of the larger constellation of an exhibition or artwork. This context is the frame for thinking cohesively, which is intrinsically part of curatorial methodologies, or the logic of the curatorial. This renewed position of the exhibition as object vis-à-vis the curatorial is critical to the theoretical position of postsensual aesthetics, meaning the work is construed with the assumption that something—a component—is part of a much larger constellation. The exhibition as an aesthetic form engages the object's latent contents, making it contemporary by taking advantage of the connective tissues among knowledge, lived experience, and the aesthetic form via the exhibition object. Aesthetic experience, through Adorno's exact imagination, is thus renewed and brought forward to act in service to postsensual aesthetics.

I want to return to the epistemological crisis in art that Carolyn Christov-Bakargiev referred to with her question, "What could the word *art* be a stand-in for?" The works by artists and curators that we have examined here aggravate meanings and, by extension, complicate expectations we have for them, however conventionally embodied. The work examined through the concept of postsensual aesthetics is reactive to a tension between the expansive activity of research, alliances among disciplines, and an interweaving of place and community that the field of contemporary art has been able to hold, even against the historical ideologies that restrain the meaning of art. At the same time, the new expectation that contemporary art has a responsibility to make meaningful and relevant contributions outside of itself—to produce knowledge that makes a difference in society—has become problematic. In his criticism of *dOCUMENTA (13)*, T. J. Demos credited the exhibition for opening up discourse around ecological issues of our time, but faulted it because it "exemplifies the failure to do anything about the very issues it raised—as if mere knowledge production releases us from any responsibility for doing things differently at the curatorial level."[5] While contemporary art has been able to absorb and hold these expansive approaches to research and knowledge production, that very position has over time placed responsibilities on it to function as a salve for the problems of the world. As Tom Holert observes,

> A central demand, voiced in various sections of public culture and addressed to the artists, has become the call to work on appropriate, adequate, and timely responses to historical events, political change, social crises, or environmental catastrophes. For it is demanded of "responsible" artists to provide fresh

> approaches to and surprising representations of such developments, rendering critique and interpretations that exhort to reflect or even revise one's moral or political standpoints. Delivering the "right" questions and unexpected, hence aesthetic "solutions" to issues conceived as "pressing"—concerning the well-being of national societies or specific communities—implies a whole gamut of preconceptions about the role of the arts in society, as well as the ethical, political, psychological, and epistemological conditions of artistic production.[6]

There was a hint of urgency in Holert's statement even as early as 2012 when he published it. The tension between competing ideologies to engage the world without purpose and to address given urgent issues with "solutions" has, in fact, rapidly evolved since then into an epistemological crisis for contemporary art. Contemporary art as a function for the production of useful, applicable knowledge has the potential to become another operative in the cultural logic of capitalism. The framework of post-sensual aesthetics is not intended to become another ideology with prescribed sets of behaviors. Nor is it intended to ascribe new meanings to art and curating. It is certainly not a discipline. In fact, we need to unlearn, leave disciplinary thought boundaries behind. I see postsensualism as a step toward more accurately recognizing and describing practices that push productively at the limits of art, exhibition, and institution. These practices can push at the limits of what is interpreted as artist and curator. The epistemological crisis, then, is not about rejecting terms like "research" but resignifying them.[7] This is, after all, what Christov-Bakargiev implies when she asks if the word "art" can be used to mean something else. And Chus Martínez also explores this crisis when recommending that research be reconditioned with new meaning. The challenge posed to these terms itself speaks to the refusal to accept ideology, but to renegotiate and reexamine the boundaries of what is possible.

Each of these cases—whether art, exhibition, or institution object—represents a way of rehearsing a field of contemporary art as a site of knowledge production, not through a single work but through the relations staged and contextualized among constellations of nodal activity. Each is also about the spaces beyond exhibition, beyond the visual where this engagement occurs, beyond objecthood. They all are about the space of cognition. What we can identify in all of the works examined here is not a set of protocols attempting to represent something or to drive home an argument, in the traditional academic sense. Instead, they offer ways of organizing information, ideas, and concepts inside frameworks made possible by what we have examined as the curatorial. The curatorial finds ways of entering conceptually into contemporary urgencies, rather than merely commenting on them. It does not deploy them as a theme or thesis. There are no hypotheses. It does not illustrate them. Instead, it embodies them. It creates events of knowledge out of them, rather than a representation of politics or a representation of activism.[8]

In response to the common, now ubiquitous, tendency in contemporary curating to routinely "address," "explore," "examine," and "interrogate" deteriorating and precarious social and urban infrastructures and the accompanying ecological failures, Irit Rogoff recommends, "Rather than protest them, we need to learn about them, understand their workings and intervene in them. So, it is *research* and not activism, communitarianism, or protest—a need to know, differently and from another perspective, and to communicate that knowledge and share it in imaginative, enticing, sociable, and compelling ways that draw one in rather than keeping people at a distance, lecturing facts at one another."[9]

Contemporaneity, as developed out of the curatorial, allows us to reconsider wider notions of periodization and historicization, and to revisit the age of the singular narrative of a thing, an artist, or a culture. Contemporaneity, if considered under this light, reflects a process of unlearning instead of learning. It insists on a new set of relations among epistemologies.

These discursive frameworks activate the contemporaneity of archives and give agency to audiences to see the elements of a constellation, to identify *a* conclusion from them, not *the* conclusion. Epistemological crisis does not necessarily force us to choose between different definitions. It allows the curatorial to be a staging ground for developing ideas. The key is to see knowledge not as we have been trained to see it. The curatorial as a concept and practice resignifies how one can arrive at knowledge in and through the field of art while prompting a reconsideration of what knowledge—what knowing—even is.

While the field of art holds contemporary art accountable to these multiple facets of being art, it does not consider the aesthetic dimensions of the contemporary art exhibition or, by extension, how they can be applied to being an institution. We need to recognize that art and the artist figure have evolved into subjects of aesthetic ideologies through the historical trajectory of their own subjectivity. Art and the artist function as representations of the ideas of art and artist, which do not always meet the realities of contemporary life. If we acknowledge these realities, we may in turn open expansive possibilities for new kinds of creative and cognitive practitioners, industries, and disciplines that can enter and work through other kinds of aesthetic contours and discourses in the expanded and generous space that contemporary art offers.

Adorno might advocate for this route, not necessarily the functionalizing of knowledge from art, but the systemic disruption—the disintegration—it poses to the ideologies of art. He would certainly not advocate for resolving the tensions between aesthetics and practice or recommend that practice become only theoretical. We learn from Adorno that there are no absolutes, no universalisms. He also teaches us to allow critical thought to shape-shift and change in order to leave possibilities for posing questions and having doubts. The idea is not to reconcile tension, but to let friction live and gain traction. If resolution is not the goal for Adorno, then perhaps the conflicts and problems introduced by what he called the culture industry, alongside the increased friction against and challenges to what art is and how it functions today, are productive problems.

The artistic and curatorial methodologies traced in this book offer a way to pause and take stock of work that continues to pull away from traditional aesthetics. Postsensual aesthetics seeks to point to a framework for describing modes of contemporary artistic and curatorial production as they relate to research and knowledge production, amplifying the broad range of aesthetic activity by an equally wide range of figures from different disciplines that contribute to the field of contemporary art. The framework seeks to take into account the role of cognition as ideas shuttle in and through contemporary art, as the exhibition form extends into other forms of public address, such as a publication, beyond the site of presentation. The theoretical framework of postsensual aesthetics seeks to broaden dialogue on the aesthetic dimensions of the exhibition form as it relates to the methodologies of the curatorial, furthering debates in aesthetics as they grapple with the continued turning away from the sensual and toward cognitive experiences in contemporary art.

ACKNOWLEDGMENTS

I am indebted to the MIT Press, in particular Victoria Hindley, who provided critical feedback and insightful reflection on an early draft of a manuscript that became *Postsensual Aesthetics*. I greatly appreciate the opportunity—now a second time—to work with the talented editorial, design, and marketing team at the MIT Press, including Matthew Abbate, Molly Seamans, and Paula Woolley.

I'm grateful to John Ewing whose thoughtful copyediting at an early stage of the manuscript helped bring the book to reality. I am deeply appreciative to the three anonymous reviewers who provided important recommendations in response to the book proposal. And while I am responsible for what is written, this book is a better work because of the time and attention they gave the manuscript

Ideas presented in this book have developed after many years of experiencing and witnessing the increasing number of cases where books and reading have become essential parts of contemporary artworks and exhibitions. I am indebted to the artists, curators, and writers whose work I've encountered and had the privilege of studying for this book, with gratitude especially to those and their associates who corresponded and met with me: Amy Balkin, Ute Meta Bauer, Heman Chong, Maria Eichhorn, Bettina Funcke, Maria Lind, Anna Lovechhio, Ben Mohai, Shierry Weber Nicholsen, Karin Oen, and Claire Pentecost.

I give thanks to the Graham Foundation for a Research Grant and the French-American Cultural Exchange / Étant Donnés Contemporary Art for a Curatorial Research Grant, both of which were immensely instrumental for initial research on the book.

My boyfriend, Nate Padavick, has been with me on numerous visits to exhibitions, museums, and biennials followed by countless conversations about contemporary art over the years. He has been an essential sounding board for reflecting on the dissonances between the claims made by art and exhibitions and the realities experienced.

NOTES

Prelude

1 Maria Eichhorn commissioned the historian Anja Heuss, who specializes in provenance research, to investigate fifteen paintings in the collection of the Städtische Galerie im Lenbachhaus in Munich. The paintings were considered "national loans," part of a massive stock of art and craft objects that had been confiscated and placed into storage by the Nazis during World War II; they were discovered by the American Military Government after the war. Documentation was insufficient for Heuss to trace the history of every painting. The research was conducted as part of the exhibition *Maria Eichhorn. Restitutionspolitik / Politics of Restitution*, curated by Susanne Gaensheimer, Kunstbau of Städtische Galerie im Lenbachhaus, Munich, November 29, 2003–February 22, 2004. See Yilmaz Dziewior, ed., *Maria Eichhorn. Catalogue Raisonné, 1986–2015* (Bregenz: Kunsthaus Bregenz, 2017), 414–419. See also Alexander Alberro, "Specters of Provenance: National Loans, the Königsplatz, and Maria Eichhorn's 'Politics of Restitution,'" *Grey Room* 18 (Winter 2004): 64–81. Alberro's illuminating analysis is an expanded version of his essay published in the catalog for the Munich exhibition.

2 The seminar, which occurred on November 18, 2015, at Haus der Kulturen der Welt (HKW), is one of several interrelated components composing the work titled *Maria Eichhorn. In den Zelten 4/5/5a/6/7/8/9/9a/10, Kronprinzenufer 29/30, Beethovenstrasse 1/2/3 (1832 to 1959) > John-Foster-Dulles-Allee 10 (since 1959), Berlin. In den Zelten*... consisted of the use of a space in the HKW, room K7, and a nameplate; a floor drawing made with white tape traversing interior and exterior spaces mapped the original boundaries of plots of land on which the HKW sits at John-Foster-Dulles-Allee 10, Berlin (typography on the tape relayed basic information about plot numbers, cadaster numbers, and addresses); and texts by Maria Eichhorn, Arno Löbbecke, and Anh-Linh Ngo for a publication produced on *In den Zelten*... The publication collects and presents an extraordinary amount of archival research about changes in ownership of the plots now occupied by HKW. It reproduces historic excerpts from

the cadaster as well as documents from the land registry, Berlin Mitte District Court, and Berlin Federal State Archive. Eichhorn's work *In den Zelten*... was part of the exhibition *Wohnungsfrage*, curated by Jesko Fezer, Nikolaus Hirsch, Wilfried Kuehn, and Hila Peleg, Haus der Kulturen der Welt, Berlin, October 23–December 14, 2015. See the publication produced by Maria Eichhorn on the occasion of the exhibition: *Maria Eichhorn. In den Zelten 4/5/5 a/6/7/8/9/9a/10, Kronprinzenufer 29/30, Beethovenstrasse 1/2/3 (1832 to 1959) > John-Foster-Dulles-Allee 10 (since 1959), Berlin* (Berlin; Haus der Kulturen der Welt, Berlin, 2015). See also Dziewior, *Maria Eichhorn*, 514–518.

3 Eichhorn worked with two researchers of architecture and urban planning Arno Löbbecke and Anh-Linh Ngo. Their study of documents from the land registry archive revealed that the land on which HKW sits—originally composed of several individual plots—was unjustly transferred from its Jewish owners under the political and social circumstances of the Nazi regime. "In den Zelten 10," for example, belonged to Magnus Hirschfeld, the sex science researcher who ran his Institute for Sexual Science in a building on this plot, which he purchased in 1920, and later in an additional building on a neighboring plot he purchased in 1921. Both served as the home of the institute until 1933 when it was plundered by the Nazis and closed by Berlin's police commissioner. Eventually, in 1936, the land was transferred to the Prussian State as the new owner. Löbbecke and Ngo describe in a text published as part of Eichhorn's *In den Zelten*... how restitution claims by heirs and the Jewish Trust Corporation were dismissed following the Second World War. See Eichhorn, *Maria Eichhorn. In den Zelten*...

4 *Rose Valland Institute*'s website states that it is "an independent interdisciplinary artistic project by Maria Eichhorn" and that the project builds upon "insights gained from Maria Eichhorn's previous exhibition projects *Restitutionspolitik / Politics of Restitution* (2003) and *In den Zelten*... (2015)." See *Rose Valland Institute*, http://www.rosevallandinstitut.org/about.html, accessed August 7, 2022.

5 The *Rose Valland Institute* cooperated with the Käte Hamburger Center "Law as Culture" program at the University of Bonn from October 2018 to March 2020. Since April 2020, the *Rose Valland Institute* has been part of the Berlin Artistic Research Grant Program.

6 In a conversation with me, Maria Eichhorn said that the Käte Hamburger Center offered the *Rose Valland Institute* support in the form of an office, staff, and funds to conduct research. The *Institute* continues to function with support from the Berlin Artistic Research Grant Program, but at time of writing it operates at less capacity than when originally founded, with one staff member conducting archival research. Author's conversation with Maria Eichhorn, August 19, 2021, New York City.

7 The most comprehensive publication on Maria Eichhorn's vast body of work is Dziewior, *Maria Eichhorn. Catalogue Raisonné, 1986–2015*, published in association with her exhibition at Kunsthaus Bregenz from May 10 to July 6, 2014.

8 In 1998, the international Washington Conference on Holocaust-Era Assets reopened the issue of restitution with a set of principles to assist participating nations in resolving questions related to Nazi-looted cultural assets.

9 Jacques Rancière, *Aesthetics and Its Discontents*, trans. Steven Corcoran (Cambridge, UK: Polity Press, 2009), 8. This is one of many instances in Rancière's philosophical writings where he uses the phrase "aesthetic regime of art."

10 Maria Lind, "The Curatorial," *Artforum* 68, no. 2 (October 2009): 103. An original version of the text is printed in *Selected Maria Lind Writing*, ed. Brian Kuan Wood (Berlin: Sternberg Press, 2010), 57–66.

11 The 2008 edition presented 54 works by 41 artists from 20 countries. The preceding 27th Bienal in 2006 included 118 artists, 645 works of art, from 51 countries, while the subsequent 29th Bienal in 2010 featured 159 artists, 850 works of art, and 40 countries. See Fundação Bienal de São Paulo, http://www.bienal.org.br/exposicoes, accessed August 7, 2022.

12 Jens Hoffmann and Maria Lind, "To Show or Not to Show," *Mousse Magazine*, no. 31 (November 2011), https://www.moussemagazine.it/magazine/jens-hoffmann-maria-lind-2011/, accessed August 7, 2022. After naming the concept in 2009, Lind continued to develop and refine the idea in interviews like this one with Hoffmann, as well as in a series of seminars at the University of Gothenburg from 2010 to 2011; a March 2011 symposium titled "History, Immateriality, and Mediation: How Can We Practice 'the Curatorial' Today?"; and an edited publication titled *Performing the Curatorial: Within and Beyond Art*, resulting from and extending exchanges at the University of Gothenburg events. See Maria Lind, ed., *Performing the Curatorial: Within and Beyond Art* (Tensta: Tensta konsthall; Gothenburg: University of Gothenburg; Berlin: Sternberg Press, 2012). See also Maria Lind, "Situating the Curatorial," *e-flux journal* 116 (March 2021), https://www.e-flux.com/journal/116/378689/situating-the-curatorial/, accessed August 7, 2022.

13 Maria Lind served as director of Tensta konsthall, Stockholm, from 2011 to 2018.

14 Simon Sheikh, "Thinking with Exhibitions, Thinking with People," in *What Museums Do: The Curatorial in Parallax*, ed. Choi Jina and Helen Jungyeon Ku (Seoul: National Museum of Modern and Contemporary Art, 2018), 162.

15 Tom Holert, *Knowledge Beside Itself: Contemporary Art's Epistemic Politics* (Berlin: Sternberg Press, 2020), 11. This book represents Holert's ongoing commitment to criticism on

artistic research and knowledge production. Two related texts: Tom Holert and Mick Wilson, "Latent Essentialisms: An e-mail Exchange on Art, Research and Education," in *Curating and the Educational Turn*, ed. Paul O'Neill and Mick Wilson (London: Open Editions, 2010), 320–328; and Tom Holert, "Being Concerned? Scattered Thoughts on 'Artistic Research' and 'Social Responsibility,'" in *Intellectual Birdhouse: Artistic Practice as Research*, ed. Ute Meta Bauer, Florian Dombois, Claudia Mareis, and Michael Schwab (London: Koenig Books, 2012), 23–39.

16 Sofía Hernández Chong Cuy, "What about Collecting?," in *Ten Fundamental Questions of Curating*, ed. Jens Hoffmann (Milan: Mousse Publishing, 2013), 62.

17 Holert, *Knowledge Beside Itself*, 8–9.

18 Holert, *Knowledge Beside Itself*, 9.

19 This is the case for Maria Eichhorn, who spoke with me about the tower of books exhibited in *documenta 14* and the stack of 500 euro notes totaling 50,000 euros exhibited in *Documenta11* in 2002. They are points for people to enter the work and from there take what they need. If they wish, visitors have the option to spend more time with the work, to read inside the gallery or later. But the works are not conceived as a total experience, meaning Eichhorn considers that visitors will not spend equal time with each part, either inside the exhibition or beyond it. Conversation with Maria Eichhorn, August 19, 2021.

20 Michael Inwood offers a useful account of the history of "aesthetics" in his introduction to *Georg Wilhelm Friedrich Hegel: Introductory Lectures on Aesthetics*, ed. Michael Inwood, trans. Bernard Bosanquet (London: Penguin Books, 2004), ix–xxxvi.

21 The typography for "documenta" uses a lower-case *d*, following the style conceived in 1955 for the first exhibition. It was a logotype envisioned to communicate the exhibition's place within the prevailing reductive simplicity of modernism. Subsequent documenta editions have interpreted the logotype "documenta" differently. Here, I italicize documenta exhibition titles that incorporate the edition number. When I refer generally to documenta, I use the lower-case *d* without italics.

22 Nicolas Bourriaud, *Relational Aesthetics*, trans. Simon Pleasance and Fronza Woods with the participation of Mathieu Copeland (Dijon: Les Presses du réel, 2002), originally published in French as *Esthétique relationnelle* by Les Presses du réel in 1998. In the book's essays, Bourriaud reflects upon works by a number of artists, many of whom were in the group exhibition *Traffic* (January 26–March 24, 1996) at the CAPC musée d'art contemporain de Bordeaux, France, where he was a visiting curator at the time.

23 Nicolas Bourriaud, *Postproduction* (Berlin: Sternberg Press, 2002), 7–8.

24 It was in the journal *Documents sur l'art*, which Bourriaud cofounded and codirected with Éric Troncy from 1992 to 2000, that many of the essays in *Relational Aesthetics* were originally published.

Section 1: *dOCUMENTA (13)*

1 As with most of the contributions to *100 Notes—100 Thoughts*, Christov-Bakargiev's letter is reproduced in *The Book of Books*. All future citations to "Letter to a Friend" refer to that source. See Carolyn Christov-Bakargiev, "Letter to a Friend, No. 003," in *dOCUMENTA (13), The Book of Books, Catalog 1/3*, ed. Carolyn Christov-Bakargiev and Chus Martínez (Ostfildern: Hatje Cantz, 2012), 74–79.

2 Carolyn Christov-Bakargiev refutes the use of "curator" to identify herself. In a conversation with Terry Smith, she says, "I would never use the word 'curator' to define myself, and I didn't call anybody who worked on *dOCUMENTA (13)* a curator.... I actually tried to liquidate this word, 'curator.' I always say 'directed.' More like a traffic controller. I actually find it a more humble, more modest term." See Terry Smith, "Carolyn Christov-Bakargiev. On Not Having an Idea: *dOCUMENTA (13)*," in *Talking Contemporary Curating*, ed. Leigh Markopoulos (New York: Independent Curators International, 2015), 43. Christov-Bakargiev is the director of the Castello di Rivoli Museo d'Arte Contemporanea and the Francesco Federico Cerruti Foundation in Turn, Italy, as well as a visiting professor at the University of Basel since 2022. She was Edith Kreeger Wolf Distinguished Visiting Professor in Art Theory and Practice at Northwestern University from 2013 to 2019. From 2016 to 2017, in Turin, she directed both the Castello di Rivoli and the GAM Civic Gallery of Modern and Contemporary Art. In 2015 she was the artistic director of the 14th Istanbul Biennale. Prior to her appointment as artistic director of *DOCUMENTA (13)* in 2008, she served as artistic director of the 16th Biennale of Sydney. She was chief curator at the Castello di Rivoli from 2001 to 2008, and from 1999 to 2002 was senior curator at MoMA PS1 in New York.

3 Bettina Funcke, former head of publications for *dOCUMENTA (13)*, recalls in an interview that, "as *dOCUMENTA (13)*'s first statement to the press, Carolyn decided to write 'Letter to a Friend' (notebook no. 003), which is thirty pages long and was sent to hundreds of journalists, most of whom were puzzled." See "Intimate Cacophonies: An Exchange Regarding *100 Notes—100 Thoughts*. Bettina Funcke and Andrew Stefan Weiner," *Fillip* 19 (Spring 2014), https://fillip.ca/content/intimate-cacophonies-an-exchange-regarding-100-notes100-thoughts, accessed August 7, 2022.

4 In a published interview between Terry Smith and Carolyn Christov-Bakargiev, Christov-Bakargiev says, "Everything in the exhibition is suggested in 'Letter to a Friend,' which was sent out

to 17,000 people in October 2010 as an attachment to the press release, but intentionally hidden in a pdf so that most people wouldn't even open it because they're afraid of computer viruses." See Smith, "On Not Having an Idea," 51.

5 Christov-Bakargiev, "Letter to a Friend," 75.

6 *dOCUMENTA (13)*, https://www.documenta.de/en/retrospective/documenta_13, accessed August 7, 2022.

7 The publication program included the 100 titles in this series, plus a three-part catalog series. *The Book of Books, Catalog 1/3*, brings together the *100 Notes* series with essays by Carolyn Christov-Bakargiev and Chus Martínez, plus information about the participants and the exhibition. It has a reading list related to the research. *The Logbook, Catalog 2/3*, coedited by Christov-Bakargiev, Bettina Funcke, and Nicola Setari (Ostfildern: Hatje Cantz, 2012), chronicles the making of *dOCUMENTA (13)* through correspondence, images, interviews, and photographic documentation of formal and informal activity from 2009 to 2012. *The Guidebook, Catalog 3/3*, coedited by Christov-Bakargiev and Bettina Funcke (Ostfildern: Hatje Cantz, 2012), has an introduction to work by artists in the exhibition and practical information about exhibition venues, programs locations, and maps.

8 She continued: "As a conventional term, it has been used to indicate an empirical and practical form of knowledge formation through the making and experience of aesthetic objects that are at once metaphors, models, and actual embodiments of how perception is elaborated into a form of knowledge and understanding in a specific place, time, and society." Christov-Bakargiev, "Letter to a Friend," 78.

9 Christov-Bakargiev remarks in an interview with Terry Smith, "I agree with you that *dOCUMENTA (13)* is also a project about curatorial practice; as I actually mentioned earlier, it's an anthology of all the modes currently in use, ranging from the most classical modernist display, like in 'The Brain,' to the idea of activist public art." See Smith, "On Not Having an Idea," 50. In her catalog essay, Christov-Bakargiev informs readers that plans for the exhibition included a proposal by the artists Guillermo Faivovich and Nicolás Goldberg to bring the second-largest meteorite in the world to Kassel in order to place it in front of the Fridericianum, the oldest museum in Europe. The 37-ton rock would have been the heaviest single object ever transported by humans. See Carolyn Christov-Bakargiev, "The dance was very frenetic, lively, rattling, clanging, rolling, contorted, and lasted a long time," in *dOCUMENTA (13), The Book of Books*, 30–31.

10 Smith, "On Not Having an Idea," 44.

11 "Agents" were recruited from across the globe to serve as advisors. They were led by Chus Martínez. In her interview with Terry Smith, Christov-Bakargiev says, "I didn't call anybody who worked on *dOCUMENTA (13)* a curator. Chus Martínez was head of a department, but we never gave the department a name." See Smith, "On Not Having an Idea," 43. The Core Agent Group was Ayreen Anastas, Rene Gabri, Marta Kuzma, Raimundas Malašauskas, Chus Martínez, Kitty Scott, and Andrea Viliani, with another group called Agents comprising Leeza Ahmady, Tue Greenfort, Sofía Hernández Chong Cuy, Sunjung Kim, Adam Kleinman, Koyo Kouoh, Joasia Krysa, Lívia Páldi, Hetti Perkins, Sarah Rifky, Eva Scharrer, and Nicolas Setari.

12 In addition to stimulating the minds of audiences about the spirit of the age, documenta was expected to stimulate the local economy while elevating Germany's international prestige in the arts. The 1955 exhibition was a success in that regard. It drew widespread media attention and 130,000 visitors during its two-month run. The economic impact on Kassel since then has turned out to be extraordinary, and the exhibition's place in the field of contemporary art unparalleled. The number of visitors has grown from 130,000 in 1955 to 905,000 in 2012, a record-setting number up 14 percent from the previous documenta in 2007. The number does not reflect the 27,000 visitors to the satellite exhibition in Kabul, Afghanistan, from June 20 to July 19, 2012; see *dOCUMENTA (13)*, https://d13.documenta.de/#/welcome/, accessed August 7, 2022. During *documenta 14*, in 2017, more than 1,230,000 people attended the exhibition, which occurred in Kassel and Athens, pouring more than €125 million into the European economy. See "*documenta 14*, First Results of a Representative Survey, September 18, 2017," https://www.documenta.de/files/Evaluation_d14_English.pdf, accessed August 7, 2022. For a historical perspective on the economics of documenta, see Christoph Lange, "The Spirit of *Documenta*: Art-Philosophical Reflections," in *Archive in Motion: 50 Jahre / Years* Documenta*, 1955–2005*, ed. Michael Glasmeier and Karen Stengel (Göttingen: Steidl, 2005).

13 Ian Wallace provides an incredibly insightful and rich account of the first *documenta* based on a lecture he presented at a symposium on early postwar art at the University of British Columbia, September 26, 1987. See Ian Wallace, "The First *documenta*, 1955," in *dOCUMENTA (13), The Book of Books*, 65–73.

14 Invoked in the preface of the catalog for the first *documenta*, written by the chief organizer Arnold Bode. Quoted in Lange, "The Spirit of *Documenta*," 14.

15 Haftmann's influence on the early mission of documenta to educate is presented and analyzed in Lange, "The Spirit of *Documenta*," 21. See also Walter Grasskamp, "For Example, *Documenta*, or, How Is Art History Produced?," in *Thinking about Exhibitions*, ed. Bruce W. Ferguson, Reesa Greenberg, and Sandy Nairne (London: Routledge, 1996), 67–78. Grasskamp examines the critical impact that Haftmann and his book *Painting in the Twentieth Century* had on the first three editions of documenta, combined with the important role of staging for Bode in narrativizing art history. Grasskamp's essay was originally published in 1982 as the introduction to volume 49 of the journal *Kunstforum International*, dedicated to the "The Myth of *documenta*: An Art Historical Picturebook."

16 See Grasskamp, "For Example, *Documenta*," 67–78; especially the section "Historicizing," in which Grasskamp discusses the extraordinary effect of Haftmann's *Painting in the Twentieth Century* on later generations of art historians and artists.

17 The attempt to elevate contemporary German modernists and situate them alongside prevailing modern masters such as Picasso was accomplished not only through Haftmann's writing about the work, but also with the exhibition installation. Bode, for example, installed a 1955 abstract work by the Kassel-based artist Fritz Winter opposite Picasso's *Girl before a Mirror* (1932), borrowed from the Museum of Modern Art. For further accounting of these exhibition design strategies, see Wallace, "The First *documenta*, 1955," 68.

18 Further to this point, in a conversation with the author, Maria Eichhorn pointed out that art historians often use primary resources, while artists and curators tend to rely on secondary resources and interpret information in less didactic, comprehensive modalities, sometimes withholding information in order to allow narratives and stories to develop within the imagination of audiences. Conversation with Maria Eichhorn, August 19, 2021, New York City.

19 Among the studies on Szeemann and *documenta 5*, my book *Beyond Objecthood: The Exhibition as a Critical Form since 1968* offers an analysis of Szeemann's curation within a history of artists and curators who looked to the exhibition as a formidable medium. See James Voorhies, *Beyond Objecthood: The Exhibition as a Critical Form since 1968* (Cambridge, MA: MIT Press, 2017).

20 For the sake of consistency, I use the term "biennial" from this point on to refer generally to the perennial, large-scale exhibition.

21 In 2003, the term "New Institutionalism" initially appeared in writing in the Office for Contemporary Art volume *Verksted #1: New Institutionalism*, edited by Jonas Ekeberg. It is both the title and subject of this first issue of *Verksted*. In her foreword, then-director Ute Meta Bauer explains: "The Office for Contemporary Art Norway could quite well be inscribed in the framework of this issue as one of the institutions that is trying to adapt to current developments in contemporary art through new means and methods. Having an open, international or, even better, transitional agenda in the area of cultural exchange requires new ways of thinking and working." See Ute Meta Bauer, foreword to "New Institutionalism," ed. Jonas Ekeberg, *Verksted* 1 (2003): 6. See also a 2007 transcript of a conversation between Alex Farquharson and Maria Lind in which they reflect on conditions related to what was being referred to at that time as New Institutionalism.

The conversation accompanied a conference titled "The New Administration of Aesthetics" held in Oslo in 2006. Maria Lind and Alex Farquharson, "Integrative Institutionalism: A Reconsideration," in *The New Administration of Aesthetics*, ed. Tone Hansen and Trude Iversen (Oslo: Torpedo, 2007), 108–125.

22 I've adopted the metaphors of dance and choreography to describe this exhibition because references to motion and performance are used throughout Christov-Bakargiev's writing about *dOCUMENTA (13)*, including the title of her essay for the main catalog. See Christov-Bakargiev, "The dance was very frenetic," 31.

23 Quoted in Elizabeth Schambelan, "Talks with Carolyn Christov-Bakargiev about *Documenta 13*," *Artforum* 50, no. 9 (May 2012).

24 Carolyn Christov-Bakargiev, "But to return to the idea of a single concept, or the absence of a single concept: It has partly to do with the resistance to the production of knowledge in a knowledge economy." See Schambelan, "Talks with Carolyn Christov-Bakargiev." Christov-Bakargiev did offer something akin to a mission statement published in the frontispiece of *The Book of Books*: "*dOCUMENTA (13)* is dedicated to artistic research and forms of imagination that explore commitment, matter, things, embodiment, and active living in connection with, yet not subordinated to, theory. These are terrains where politics are inseparable from a sensual, energetic, and worldly alliance between current research in various scientific and artistic fields and other knowledges, both ancient and contemporary. *dOCUMENTA (13)* is driven by a holistic and non-logocentric vision that is skeptical of the persisting belief in economic growth. This vision is shared with, and recognizes, the shapes and practices of knowing of all the animate and inanimate makers of the world, including people." See Christov-Bakargiev, frontispiece, *dOCUMENTA (13), The Book of Books*.

25 T. J. Demos, "Curating against the Apocalypse, *Documenta 13*, 2012," in *Curating and Politics beyond the Curator: Initial Reflections*, ed. Heidi Bale Amundsen and Gerd Elise Mørland (Ostfildern: Hatje Cantz, 2015), 75. This essay is an expanded version of Demos's "Gardens beyond Eden: Bio-aesthetics, Eco-Futurism, and Dystopia at *dOCUMENTA (13)*," *The Brooklyn Rail* (October 2012). It was later transformed into a third version as the chapter "Gardening against the Apocalypse: The Case of dOCUMENTA (13)," in T. J. Demos, *Decolonizing Nature: Contemporary Art and the Politics of Ecology* (Berlin: Sternberg Press, 2016).

26 Leftloft was responsible for the graphic design and branding of *dOCUMENTA (13)*. They developed a combination of lower-case and upper-case typographical character schemes using numbers inside brackets. In a conversation with Bettina Funcke (New York City, April 27, 2021), she told me the combination was intended to make it challenging to actually type the name. Also, the design identity for *dOCUMENTA (13)* is a refusal to visually fix the graphic identity for the exhibition, almost a kind of non-identity identity, or as stated on Leftloft's website: "The words dOCUMENTA (13) [are] not a logo, but a theoretical concept contained in a typographical shrewdness. The case-sensitive inversion can be represented freely, with any font and even hand-written: it will always be a universally recognizable symbol which expresses the reversal of the order and a dynamic desire for renewal." Lefloft, https://leftloft.com/case-study/documenta-13/, accessed August 7, 2022. For more on the important role that graphic design, branding, typography, and communication have historically played since the first *documenta*, see Kathryn M. Floyd, "d is for documenta: Institutional Identity for a Periodic Exhibition," in "*documenta*. Curating the History of the Present," ed. Nanne Buurman and Dorothee Richter, special issue, *ONCURATING.org* 33 (June 2017): 9–19, https://www.on-curating.org/files/oc/dateiverwaltung/issue-33/pdf/Oncurating_Issue33.pdf, accessed August 7, 2022. See also Ian Wallace's analysis of Arnold Bode's attention to graphic design for the first *documenta*, where the simple shape of a lower-case, sans-serif *d* was chosen to signify modernity. Wallace, "The First *documenta*, 1955," 65–73.

27 For a comprehensive and insightful discussion on *100 Notes—100 Thoughts*, see "Intimate Cacophonies."

28 Christov-Bakargiev, "Letter to a Friend," 78.

29 Demos, "Curating against the Apocalypse," 86. I want to emphasize that while I have selected this essay by Demos to include in my argument, it is not an isolated case, either for Demos, who often advocates for work by artists whose urgencies align with political and activist imperatives, or for numerous other critics, curators, and artists whose advocacy has a stake in the social and political function of art. See also T. J. Demos, "Life Full of Holes," *Grey Room* 24 (Summer 2006): 72–87; reprinted in *The Green Room: Reconsidering the Documentary and Contemporary Art*, ed. Maria Lind and Hito Steyerl (Annandale-on-Hudson: Center for Curatorial Studies Bard College; Berlin: Sternberg Press, 2008), 104–126.

30 Demos, "Curating against the Apocalypse," 75.

31 Demos, "Curating against the Apocalypse," 80.

32 Phone conversation with Claire Pentecost, May 4, 2021.

33 Their collaboration resulted in the work presented at *dOCUMENTA (13)* and in booklet No. 009 of the *100 Notes* series.

34 *The Return of a Lake* (Köln: Walther König, 2012) features texts by Maria Thereza Alves, Catalina Lozano, and Raúl Vázquez Palacios. In addition to Alves's book, *dOCUMENTA (13)* published nine books (most in partnership with Walther König or Hatje Cantz) as part of artists' participation in the exhibition: Guillermo Faivovich and Nicolás Goldberg, *The Campo del Cielo Meteorites*, vol. 1, *El Taco*, with texts by Daniel Birnbaum, Simon Starling, and Carolyn Christov-Bakargiev (Ostfildern: Hatje Cantz, 2011); Guillermo Faivovich and Nicolás Goldberg, *The Campo del Cielo Meteorites*, vol. 2, *El Chaco*, with texts by Graciela Speranza, Etel Adnan, and William A. Cassidy (Köln: Walther König, 2013); *Natascha Sadr Haghighian: Trail*, ed. Jasper Kettner, Pola Sieverding, with texts by Reza Abedini, Daniel Berndt, Binna Choi, Reza Haeri, et al. (Leipzig: Spector Books, 2016); *Füsun Onur*, with texts by Defne Ayas and a conversation among Carolyn Christov-Bakargiev, Hans Ulrich Obrist, and Füsun Onur (Köln: Walther König, 2013); Theaster Gates, *12 Ballads for Huguenot House*, with texts by Carolyn Christov-Bakargiev, Madeleine Grynsztejn, Michael Darling, Theaster Gates, Matthew Jesse Jackson, and John Preus (Köln: Walther König; published in partnership with the Museum of Contemporary Art, Chicago, 2012); John Menick, *A Report on the City* (Köln: Walther König, 2012); Nalini Malani, *In Search of Vanished Blood*, with texts by Carolyn Christov-Bakargiev, Andreas Huyssen, and Livia Monnet (Ostfildern: Hatje Cantz, 2012); *Dora García, Klau Mich, Mad Marginal Number 3*, with texts by Carolyn Christov-Bakargiev, Yolanda Romero, Claire Bishop, Ellen Blumenstein, Eva Fabbris, Chus Martínez, and Carmen Roll (Köln: Walther König, 2013). I'm indebted to Bettina Funcke for drawing my attention to these titles.

35 The sale was executed on June 16, 2004. Balkin purchased 24 pounds of 2003 cycle 2, zone 1 NO_X Reclaim Trading Credits at $4.25 per pound, equaling $102.00.

36 As a UNESCO State Party, Germany was invited to lead a coalition process. Germany's Federal Ministry for the Environment, Nature Conservation, and Nuclear Safety replied, stating that Germany would not lead a coalition for inscription.

37 By the close of *dOCUMENTA (13)*, almost 100,000 postcards were completed and mailed to the Federal Environment Minister in Germany. Skype conversation with Amy Balkin, April 14, 2021.

38 Admittedly, knowing more about Koons's work before experiencing it can provide viewers greater insight into its conceptual underpinnings, but that knowledge isn't integral to how the work is conceived and intended to be experienced.

39 Tom Holert's book *Knowledge Beside Itself: Contemporary Art's Epistemic Politics* (Berlin: Sternberg Press, 2020) offers a valuable and insightful analysis of knowledge production in the contemporary arts. See, especially, "Introduction: Contemporary Art and the Traffic-Driven Episteme," in Holert, *Knowledge Beside Itself*, 6–61.

40 Dieter Mersch, "Aesthetic Thinking: Art as *theōria*," in *Aesthetic Theory*, ed. Dieter Mersch, Sylvia Sasse, and Sandro Zanetti (Zurich: DIAPHANES, 2019), 233.

41 The reference to knowledge as "an event" is made by practitioners such as Irit Rogoff and Jean-Paul Martinon. See for example, "Irit Rogoff: The Exhibition as an Event of Knowledge Production," lecture, Asia Art Archive, October 2013, https://aaa.org.hk/en/programmes/programmes/irit-rogoff-the-exhibition-as-an-event-of-knowledge-production, accessed August 7, 2022; and Jean-Paul

Martinon, introduction to Jean-Paul Martinon, ed., *The Curatorial: A Philosophy of Curating* (London: Bloomsbury, 2013), 1–13.

42 In her writing and interviews, Christov-Bakargiev often talks about doubt and skepticism as productive agents for seeking truth within the context of research. See, for example, Christov-Bakargiev, "The dance was very frenetic," 36–37; and "Worlding Matter: A Dialogue with Carolyn Christov-Bakargiev," in *Reclaiming Artistic Research*, ed. Lucy Cotter (Berlin: Hatje Cantz, 2019), 251–252. In addition, in his contribution to *100 Notes*, Bifo-Franco Berardi talks about the place of skepticism as part of a reevaluation of what is understood as truth. See Berardi, "Ironic Ethic," in *dOCUMENTA (13), The Book of Books*, 204–207.

43 Conversation with Maria Eichhorn, New York City, August 19, 2021.

44 Further to this point, a magisterial essay by Chus Martínez offers an astute critique of artistic research and meaning. See Chus Martínez, "How a Tadpole Becomes a Frog: Belated Aesthetics, Politics, and Animated Matter. Toward a Theory of Artistic Research," in *dOCUMENTA (13), The Book of Books*, 46–57.

45 Christov-Bakargiev, "Letter to a Friend," 75.

46 Paul O'Neill and Mick Wilson's contributions to this discourse on the discursive turns toward research and to expansive approaches of the curatorial are many, including titles in the Occasional Table series for Open Editions / de Appel. O'Neill's *The Culture of Curating and the Curating of Culture(s)* also situates experimental approaches to curating within broader philosophical and contemporary art trajectories including the legacy of conceptual art. See O'Neill, *The Culture of Curating and the Curating of Culture(s)* (Cambridge, MA: MIT Press, 2012).

47 The reviews are numerous in praise and criticism. A selection of reviews referred to the challenge of being able to experience and comprehend the entire exhibition. These include: Roberta Smith, "Art Show as Unruly Organism," *New York Times* (June 14, 2012); Daniel Birnbaum, "*Documenta 13*," *Artforum* 51, no. 4 (October 2012); H. G. Masters, "*Documenta 13*," *ArtAsiaPacific* 80 (September/October 2012); and Kathleen MacQueen, "*dOCUMENTA (13)*: When Too Much Is Not Enough," *Bomb* (August 6, 2012).

48 Since the beginning of documenta, however, books have had a surprisingly important place. Anna Sigrídur Arnar traces different approaches to incorporating publications into different editions—from inviting visitors to read and handle them in *documenta 5*, to presenting books as untouchable objects in *documenta 6*, to integrating them into the curatorial methodologies underlying *dOCUMENTA (13)* and *documenta 14*. See Anna Sigrídur Arnar, "Books at documenta: Medium, Art Object, Cultural Symbol," in "*documenta*. Curating the History of the Present," ed. Nanne Buurman and Dorothee Richter, special issue, *ONCURATING.org* 33 (June

2017): 151–164, https://www.on-curating.org/files/oc/dateiverwaltung/issue-33/pdf/Oncurating_Issue33.pdf, accessed August 7, 2022.

49 "*Genius* is the talent (or natural gift) which gives the rule to art. Since talent, as the innate productive faculty of the artist, belongs itself to nature, we may express the matter thus: Genius is the innate mental disposition (*ingenium*) *through which* nature gives the rule of art. / Whatever may be thought of this definition, whether it is merely arbitrary or whether it is adequate to the concept that we are accustomed to combine with the word *genius*, we can prove already beforehand that, according to the signification of the word here adopted, beautiful arts must necessarily be considered as arts of *genius*." Immanuel Kant, §46 "Beautiful art is the art of genius," Second Book: Analytic of the Sublime, in Kant, *Critique of Judgement*, trans. J. H. Bernard (New York: Hafner Press, 1951), 150.

50 Beatrice von Bismarck wonderfully captures the concept of the constellation as a metaphor for thinking about the interchangeable relations, and thus meanings, derivable from entities in motion, whereas "In its original scientific context, a constellation is also characterized by a spatiotemporal dynamic. Distinguishing between fixed stars and planets, the heavenly bodies linked in a constellation are assigned a specific mobility that, in turn, influences the constellation. Both as a spatial metaphor that describes the arrangement of bodies in a three-dimensional field and as a characterization of the temporal dimension that mediates between recurring and one-time movements, *constellation* refers to a changeable relational structure between individual elements, which, in turn, can change in their own right. In this way, it captures a moment in the configuration of elements that is unstable and ephemeral. Instead of a fixed formation, it denotes open-ended stages of assemblage or coming-together." See Beatrice von Bismarck, "Constellations and Transpositions: On the Political Potential of Curatorial Practice," in *What Museums Do: The Curatorial in Parallax*, ed. Choi Jina and Helen Jungyeon Ku (Seoul: National Museum of Modern and Contemporary Art, 2018), 132.

51 With one exception: the philosopher and writer Daniel Heller-Roazen did not give permission for his notebook, No. 052, to be reproduced in Christov-Bakargiev and Martínez, *dOCUMENTA (13), The Book of Books*. Conversation with Bettina Funcke, New York City, April 27, 2021.

52 Susan Buck-Morss, *The Origins of Dialectics: Theodor W. Adorno, Walter Benjamin, and the Frankfurt Institute* (New York: The Free Press, 1977), 64.

53 Martinon, "Theses in the Philosophy of Curating," in Martinon, *The Curatorial*, 26.

Interlude

1 Immanuel Kant writes, "If art which is adequate to the *cognition* of a possible object performs the actions requisite therefor merely in order to make it actual, it is *mechanical* art; but if it has for its immediate design the feeling of pleasure, it is called *aesthetical* art. This is again either *pleasant* or *beautiful*. It is the first if its purpose is that the pleasure should accompany the representations [of the object] regarded as mere *sensations*; it is the second if they are regarded as *modes of cognition*. / Pleasant arts are those that are directed merely to enjoyment.... / On the other hand, beautiful art is a mode of representation which is purposive for itself and which, although devoid of [definite] purpose, yet furthers the culture of the mental powers in reference to social communication." See Immanuel Kant, §44 "Of beautiful art," Second Book: Analytic of the Sublime, in Kant, *Critique of Judgement*, trans. J. H. Bernard (New York: Hafner Press, 1951), 148.

2 Casey Haskins provides a lucid account of Kant's categorization of art. See Casey Haskins, "Kant and the Autonomy of Art," *The Journal of Aesthetics and Art Criticism*, 47, no. 1 (winter 1989): 43–54.

3 *Critique of Pure Reason* (1781, 1787), *Critique of Practical Reason* (1788), *Critique of Judgement* (1790).

4 Theodor Adorno, "The Actuality of Philosophy" (1931), *Telos* 31 (spring 1977): 125.

5 Kant writes: "In a product of beautiful art, we must become conscious that it is art and not nature; but yet the purposiveness in its form must seem to be as free from all constraint of arbitrary rules as if it were a product of mere nature. On this feeling of freedom in the play of our cognitive faculties, which must at the same time be purposive, rests that pleasure which alone is universally communicable, without being based on concepts. Nature is beautiful because it looks like art, and art can only be called beautiful if we are conscious of it as art while yet it looks like nature." See Kant, §45 "Beautiful art is an art in so far as it seems like nature," Second Book: Analytic of the Sublime, in Kant, *Critique of Judgement*, 149.

6 See especially the introduction to Peter Uwe Hohendhal, *The Fleeting Promise of Art: Adorno's Aesthetic Theory Revisited* (Ithaca: Cornell University, Press, 2013), 1–30.

7 Susan Buck-Morss, *The Origins of Dialectics: Theodor W. Adorno, Walter Benjamin, and the Frankfurt Institute* (New York: The Free Press, 1977), 64.

8 For instance, see Adorno's "Logic of Disintegration," in Theodor W. Adorno, *Negative Dialectics*, trans. E. B. Ashton (London: Continuum, 2007), 144–146.

9 Adorno writes, "The concept of the particular is always its negation at the same time; it cuts short what the particular is and what

nonetheless cannot be directly named, and it replaces this with identity. This negative, wrong, and yet simultaneously necessary moment is the stage of dialectics. The core, which is also abstract in the idealist version, is not simply eliminated. Its distinction from 'nothing' means that—contrary to Hegel—even the most indefinite 'something' would not be downright indefinite. This refutes the idealist doctrine of the subjectivity of all definitions. The particular would not be definable without the universal that identifies it, according to current logic; but neither is it identical with the universal." Adorno, *Negative Dialectics*, 173.

10 Theodor Adorno, "Draft Introduction," in Adorno, *Aesthetic Theory*, ed. Gretel Adorno and Rolf Tiedemann, trans. Robert Hullot-Kentor (London: Continuum, 1997), 355. Adorno's use of *Gehalt* refers to the work's objective content, in other words the substance inherent in the art itself, as opposed to *Inhalt*, which is the idea associated with the art, content as something relatable, separate from its essence, which could be the plot of a play or the subject of a painting.

11 See, for instance, "Constellation," in Adorno, *Negative Dialectics*, 162–163. See also, with regard to philosophy, his 1931 lecture "The Actuality of Philosophy," where he writes, "So philosophy has to bring its elements, which it receives from the sciences, into changing constellations, or, to say it with less astrological and scientifically more current expression, into changing trial combinations, until they fall into a figure which can be read as an answer, while at the same time the question disappears." See Adorno, "The Actuality of Philosophy," 127.

12 Adorno, *Aesthetic Theory*, 356.

13 Adorno writes, "The pathway of mediation is construable in the structure of artworks, that is, in their technique. Knowledge of this leads to the objectivity of the work itself, which is so to speak vouched for by the coherence of the work's configuration. This objectivity, however, can ultimately be nothing other than the truth content. It is the task of aesthetics to trace the topography of these elements. In the authentic artwork, what is dominated—which finds expression by way of the dominating principle—is the counterpoint to the domination of what is natural or material. This dialectical relationship results in the truth content of artworks." Adorno, *Aesthetic Theory*, 285.

14 Adorno writes, "Kant's concept of what is pleasing according to its form is retrograde with regard to aesthetic experience and cannot be restored." Adorno, *Aesthetic Theory*, 355.

15 Adorno, *Aesthetic Theory*, 355.

16 Kant, "Beautiful art is a mode of representation which is purposive for itself and which, although devoid of [definite] purpose, yet furthers the culture of the mental powers in reference to social communication. / The universal communicability of a pleasure carries with it in its very concept that the pleasure is not one of enjoyment, from mere sensation, but must be derived from reflection; and thus aesthetical art, as the art of beauty, has for standard the reflective judgement and not sensation." See §44 "Of beautiful art," in Kant, *Critique of Judgement*, 148–149.

17 Adorno, *Aesthetic Theory*, 2–3.

18 Adorno, *Aesthetic Theory*, 3.

19 Quoted in Elizabeth Schambelan, "Talks with Carolyn Christov-Bakargiev about *Documenta 13*," *Artforum* 50, no. 9 (May 2012).

20 See Section 1 of this book, footnote 49, and Kant, §46 "Beautiful art is the art of genius," Second Book: Analytic of the Sublime, in Kant, *Critique of Judgement*, 150–151.

Section 2: *Documenta11*

1 A series of published essays and interviews from the early 2000s reveal the progression of Enwezor's thinking on what he called "the postcolonial constellation." See Carol Becker and Okwui Enwezor, "A Conversation with Okwui Enwezor," *Art Journal* 61, no. 2 (Summer 2002): 8–27; Okwui Enwezor, "The Black Box," in *Documenta 11_Platform 5: Exhibition Catalogue* (Ostfildern-Ruit: Hatje Cantz, 2002); Okwui Enwezor, "The Postcolonial Constellation: Contemporary Art in a State of Permanent Transition," *Research in African Literatures* 34, vol. 4 (Winter 2003): 57–82; a later version of this last essay was published with the same title in *Antinomies of Art and Culture: Modernity, Postmodernity, Contemporaneity*, ed. Terry Smith, Okwui Enwezor, and Nancy Condee (Durham, NC: Duke University Press, 2008); a 2005 interview with Paul O'Neill, "Curating Beyond the Canon: Okwui Enwezor Interviewed by Paul O'Neill," in *Curating Subjects*, ed. Paul O'Neill (London: Open Editions, 2007); Okwui Enwezor, "Modernity and Postcolonial Ambivalence," in *Altermodern*, ed. Nicolas Bourriaud (London: Tate Publishing, 2009); Okwui Enwezor, "A Questionnaire on 'The Contemporary,'" *October* 130 (Fall 2009): 33–40; Terry Smith, "Okwui Enwezor. World Platforms, Exhibiting Adjacency, and the Surplus Value of Art," in *Talking Contemporary Curating*, ed. Leigh Markopoulos (New York: Independent Curators International, 2015); Okwui Enwezor, "Place-Making or in the 'Wrong Place': Contemporary Art and the Postcolonial Condition," in *Former West: Art and the Contemporary after 1989*, ed. Maria Hlavajova and Simon Sheikh (Utrecht: BAK, basis voor actuele kunst; Cambridge, MA: MIT Press, 2016). In addition, Terry Smith's contribution to the Platform 6 website offers a contextual analysis of Enwezor's theory of the postcolonial constellation in relation to his work on *Documenta11*. See Terry Smith, "Exhibiting the Postcolonial Constellation," Platform 6, https://www.documenta-platform6.de, accessed August 7, 2022.

2 This point is made in his response to the *October* questionnaire on contemporary art: "We need to *provincialize modernism*, that

is, to spatialize it as a series of local modernisms rather than one big universal modernism. If there is no one lineage of modernism or, for that matter, of contemporary art, then to fully grasp its qualities of historical reflection requires a heterotemporal understanding." See Enwezor, "A Questionnaire on 'The Contemporary,'" 36.

3 Enwezor, "The Postcolonial Constellation," 69.

4 Enwezor, "The Postcolonial Constellation," 59.

5 In a 2005 interview with Paul O'Neill, Enwezor says, "I make no secret of the fact that I was very interested in the post-colonial dimension of *Documenta11*, and I mean the most expansive way that one could understand it. The post-colonial is not simply the elsewhere, over there, and over here means something else, but to see the entire global entanglement as post-colonial in its shape." In O'Neill, "Curating Beyond the Canon," 113.

6 Ute Meta Bauer refers to Enwezor's reaction when he was described as the first non-European curator; she remarked that he said he was actually the first "African curator." See "Meeting Worlds: On Okwui Enwezor's Work," online video panel organized by the New Museum in association with the exhibition *Grief and Grievance*, January 21, 2021, https://vimeo.com/505808260, accessed August 7, 2022.

7 Basualdo is from Argentina; Bauer is the first woman from Germany to co-curate documenta; Ghez is from the United States; Maharaj, who was born in South Africa, is of Indian descent; Nash is from the United Kingdom; and Zaya is from the Canary Islands, which are geographically part of Africa. In an interview with Paul O'Neill, Enwezor remarked, "I wanted to emphatically make it clear in the context of *Documenta11* that there was no single author but a group of collaborators very much in turn with each other's strengths and weaknesses.... I deliberately chose people who were not all curators by profession. I wanted to have a mixture of intelligences, if you will, within the group and I couldn't have been blessed with a better group of people." See O'Neill, "Curating Beyond the Canon," 117. Anthony Gardner and Charles Green offer an analysis of the importance of this curatorial team's academic and curatorial training and their impact on the exhibition. See Anthony Gardner and Charles Green, "Post-North? *Documenta11* and the Challenges of the 'Global Exhibition,'" in "*documenta*. Curating the History of the Present," ed. Nanne Buurman and Dorothee Richter, special issue, *ONCURATING.org* 33 (June 2017): 109–121, https://www.on-curating.org/files/oc/dateiverwaltung/issue-33/pdf/Oncurating_Issue33.pdf, accessed August 7, 2022.

8 Some reviewers, such as David Galloway in the *New York Times*, pointed out that while 115 artists participated in the exhibition, "Most of the show's Third World participants live in Europe or America and have frequently lent an exotic touch to international exhibitions." Enwezor chose to have more works by fewer artists compared to previous editions of documenta, and yet the artists hailed from a significantly greater geographic range than earlier editions. Galloway states, "this is the smallest show in Documenta history. Even the inaugural, improvised presentation of 1955 spotlighted no fewer than 148 artists, while Documenta 8 went off the graph with works by 412 artists from 24 countries. But Enwezor's roster of 115 embraces 45 countries, and it sprawls across more territory than any of its predecessors, thanks to the acquisition of a gigantic hall in a former brewery." David Galloway, "Documenta 11: The Retro-ethno-techno Exhibition: The Silence Is Broken in Kassel," *New York Times*, June 15, 2002. Note, however, that *Documenta11*'s website records 117 artists participated in the exhibition. Galloway's count likely referred to an earlier published press release. See *Documenta11*, https://www.documenta.de/en/retrospective/documenta11, accessed August 7, 2022.

9 Gardner and Green remark on the significance of Enwezor's choice of the term "platform" because of its multiple meanings, including "a manifesto, a rhetorical gesture and an outline of a plan for the future." See Gardner and Green, "Post-North?," 113.

10 In her insightful chronicle of experimental curatorial practice of the 1990s, Kate Fowle cites a 2010 study revealing that thirty-two biennials were launched in the 1990s compared to twenty-seven in a period of almost 100 years between Venice's launch in 1895 and 1989 (the year of the fall of the Berlin Wall, marking a radical shift in globalization). See Kate Fowle, "Action Research: Generative Curatorial Practice," in *Curatorial Research*, ed. Paul O'Neill and Mick Wilson (London: Open Editions, 2015), 154.

11 In an interview with Terry Smith, Enwezor remarks: "I've gone on record repeatedly to defend biennials.... Not all biennials can be weighed together, but because of their cyclical nature and their immediacy exhibition makers are able to react, respond, and address some of these questions. They can challenge some of the conventions that we find in museums, especially their function as canonical passageways through which everything has to pass. The extreme contingency of biennials is highly productive for enabling us to think about the various genealogies of contemporary art. This does not happen sufficiently in commercial galleries, or in museums." See Smith, "World Platforms," 100.

12 Reflecting on Enwezor's accomplishments after his death in 2019, Jörg Heiser wrote in *Frieze*, "His thematic group exhibitions...set him apart from a class of curators mainly thriving on associating themselves with big solo names and shows, instead continuously proposing thematic group shows and constellations that redefined art history well into the present in the wake of post-colonial and decolonial thought, while pushing the envelope of what should be accepted as the 'canon.'" Jörg Heiser, "How Curator Okwui Enwezor (1963–2019) Changed the Course of Art," *Frieze* 203 (March 2019), https://www.frieze.com/article/how-curator-okwui-enwezor-1963-2019-changed-course-art, accessed August 7, 2022.

13 Enwezor, "Place-Making or in the 'Wrong Place,'" 54. Enwezor juxtaposed newspaper clippings, music, and archival objects against the art in order to set the entire exhibition within a wider cultural context.

14 Gardner and Green write that Enwezor's earlier curatorial projects had, indeed, laid the groundwork for what he would do with *Documenta11*, observing, "The main thrust of Enwezor's argument at Johannesburg was already that contemporary globalization politically and conceptually relates to historical colonialism, and that an examination of the enduring cultural mélange formed by colonialism 'breathes new life' into thinking about globalization." See Gardner and Green, "Post-North?," 110. See also Natasha Becker, "In the Wake of Okwui Enwezor," *Nka: Journal of Contemporary African Art* 48 (May 2021): 14–22.

15 Enwezor, "Place-Making or in the 'Wrong Place,'" 53.

16 Enwezor told Paul O'Neill in 2005: "One other thing I want to add is the degree to which the contemporary curator really began to undo the power of the critic in this sense. That is really a story that still needs to be told in a way. We cannot possibly say clearly why it happened, but it did happen, but it appears to me that it came about as a reaction to the power of the critic as the arbiter of meaning. Think of Clement Greenberg and to a lesser extent the criticism that currently emanate from *October*. While in the past, it was difficult to ignore these authorities; today the insurgency of the curator of contemporary art has shifted the scope of the critic's power.... As much as we want to deny that, all this has helped shape the very work of the contemporary curator and I believe that my work is part of this trajectory." O'Neill, "Curating Beyond the Canon," 111.

17 Enwezor, "The Black Box," 42–43.

18 Enwezor remarks, "It is of significant interest to see in the curator a figure who has assumed a position as a producer of certain kinds of thought about art, artists, exhibitions, and ideas and their place among a field of other possible forms of thought that govern the transmission and reception of artistic production; to think reflexively also about museums." See Enwezor, "The Postcolonial Constellation," 76.

19 Enwezor told Paul O'Neill in 2005, "For us the question was how do we read the map of contemporary art from Kassel and that meant that Kassel had to be connected to these vectors. That is how the 'Platforms' emerged. Of course, this was the original idea that I had, that I presented to the nominating committee in 1998 in Berlin. We wanted to look at the notion of the canon. We wanted to look at different ways of working." See O'Neill, "Curating Beyond the Canon," 118.

20 Further to this point, Simon Sheikh outlines a helpful taxonomy of different approaches to artistic and curatorial research for exhibition making as they relate to different kinds of sociological, journalistic, and scientific research methodologies and disciplines, when he writes, "The curatorial project—including its most dominant form, the exhibition—should thus not only be thought of as a form of mediation of research but also as a site for carrying out this research, as a place for enacted research." See Simon Sheikh, "Towards the Exhibition as Research," in *Curating Research*, ed. Paul O'Neill and Mick Wilson (London: Open Editions, 2015), 40.

21 Ute Meta Bauer, "The Space of *Documenta11*: *Documenta11* as a Zone of Activity," in *Documenta 11_Platform 5: Exhibition Catalogue* (Ostfildern-Ruit: Hatje Cantz, 2002), 103.

22 *Documenta11*'s website states that 117 artists participated in the exhibition. *Documenta11*, https://www.documenta.de/en/retrospective/documenta11, accessed August 7, 2022. See also note 8 in this section.

23 Catherine David's 1997 edition of documenta, *Documenta X*, was, without a doubt, an exhibition of global contemporary art. The contributions to these discourses by *Documenta X* are expansive and wide-reaching, representative, too, of the changing conditions of the biennial exhibitionary complex and deserving of critical analysis beyond the scope of this book.

24 For Enwezor, Western supremacism is the "sphere of global totality that manifests itself through the political, social, economic, cultural, juridical, and spiritual integration achieved via institutions devised and maintained solely to perpetuate the influence of European and North American modes of being. Two chief attributes of this integration are to be seen in the constitution of the first and second phases of modernity: firstly, in the far-reaching effects of the world system of capitalism and the state form; secondly, in the perpetual interpretation of what a just society ought to be, pursued through the secular vision of democracy as the dominant principle of political participation." See Enwezor, "The Black Box," 46.

25 Bauer, "The Space of *Documenta11*," 103.

26 I do not address two books from this group: the *Documenta11: Urban Imaginaries from Latin America*, edited by Armando Silva, and *Documenta11_Platform 5: Exhibition. Short Guide.*

27 *Documenta 11_Platform 5: Exhibition Catalogue* (Ostfildern-Ruit: Hatje Cantz, 2002) and *Documenta 11_Platform 5: Exhibition Venues* (Ostfildern-Ruit: Hatje Cantz, 2002).

28 "Meeting Worlds: On Okwui Enwezor's Work."

29 See "Meeting Worlds: On Okwui Enwezor's Work." Further to this point about the Binding-Brauerei, in a conversation with me at the Canadian Centre for Architecture in Montréal in 2018, Wilfried Kuehn reflected on Kuehn Malvezzi's work for *Documenta11* and

their design of the Binding-Brauerei, saying, "We approached this situation thinking of our work in terms of an urban layout, where you provide a spatial concept that needs to be precise without designing the architecture of a single building, because that would present too many things. . . . Following the overlap of enfilade and corridor circulation, each visitor could produce their subjective *parcours*, linking the spaces in a specific rhythm and thus producing relations between the single installations." See "Arguments, Generously Arranged: Wilfried Kuehn and James Voorhies on Shaping Relationships between Object, Idea, Setting, and Viewer," in *The Museum Is Not Enough* 1, ed. Giovanna Borasi and Albert Ferré (Montréal: Canadian Centre for Architecture; Berlin: Sternberg Press, 2019), 58.

30 As a tribute to Okwui Enwezor and to fulfill an idea discussed during the organization of *Documenta11*, a sixth *Documenta11* platform was published in April 2021. "Platform 6" is an archive and living research outlet, making available content published by *Documenta11* while hosting ongoing contributions and writings by experts and participants in the field. Platform 6 thus places *Documenta11* in dialogue with the contemporary arts. See Platform 6, https://www.documenta-platform6.de/category/enwezor/, accessed August 7, 2022.

31 In a conversation with Paul O'Neill, Enwezor remarks on the impossibility of total viewership of *Documenta11*: "We wanted to confound that. We wanted to say that it is not possible to simply absorb everything as yet another fast food meal. We wanted to make it clear, that if the public were to insist on absorbing everything then the period of digestion must by necessity take much longer to digest the material. I think we run around these exhibitions thinking that you grasp it all, but that was precisely the point and it became not only a project of endurance. That wasn't the point. It was about the impossibility of total consumption." See O'Neill, "Curating Beyond the Canon," 118.

32 Irit Rogoff, "The Expanded Field," in *The Curatorial: A Philosophy of Curating*, ed. Jean-Paul Martinon (London: Bloomsbury, 2013), 46.

33 Rogoff, "The Expanded Field," 46.

34 Tom Holert, *Knowledge Beside Itself: Contemporary Art's Epistemic Politics* (Berlin: Sternberg Press, 2020), 24.

35 Enwezor, "The Black Box," 43.

36 In an online conversation for the New Museum as part of the exhibition *Grief and Grievance*, Ute Meta Bauer comments on Enwezor's organization of *Documenta11* and his interest in representing exhibitions: "He invited complete exhibitions, [like] the late Constant's *New Babylon*; he invited the entire show from Witte de With into *Documenta11*. We had multiple entire shows: Allan Sekula's *Fish Story*, Fareed Armaly's *From/To*. We have to show the whole context, the grand narrative of each of these

shows, the dimensions of those shows, the significance of those shows, to bigger audiences." Bauer then remarks that Enwezor would say, "We have to turn art histories around and we have to turn around how they feed into politics. . . . He always placed the works in their wider political narrative." See Ute Meta Bauer's presentation (at about 35 minutes into discussion), on the panel in which she participated, "Meeting Worlds: On Okwui Enwezor's Work." Further to this point of Enwezor's interpretation of the exhibition as an object, as a total thing that could be represented and recontextualized within a given moment, he told Terry Smith in an interview in 2013 that "time should be open to revisiting, and exhibitions to re-curating. Why must certain exhibitions be done only once? If a show is relevant once, can it be relevant a second time, or third, or fourth time, as a way of really doing a review, or survey, of some significant question, some important moment, some interesting place?" See Smith, "World Platforms," 111–112.

37 These remarks were made later, in 2007, in her introduction to the book *Maria Eichhorn: Maria Eichhorn Aktiengesellschaft* published as part of Eichhorn's eponymous exhibition at the Van Abbemuseum in Eindhoven on the occasion of the work's entering the museum's collection. See Maria Eichhorn, introduction to Maria Eichhorn, *Maria Eichhorn Aktiengesellschaft*, ed. Christiane Berndes (Köln: Walther König, 2007), 23.

38 About the windows, in descriptions of each component of the work, Eichhorn states: "The windows of the exhibition hall on the first floor of the Museum Fridericianum could be opened. At the suggestion of the curator of *Documenta11* blinds were installed to darken the hall so that little light could penetrate the adjoining halls. The curator's plan was, as far as possible, for there to be no daylight in any of the *Documenta11* exhibition halls. The open windows of the *Maria Eichhorn Aktiengesellschaft* exhibition hall, on the one hand, pointed to the outside world and, on the other, continued the aesthetics of the transparent, back-lit (duratrans) document displays." See Eichhorn, introduction to *Maria Eichhorn Aktiengesellschaft*, 13. In a conversation with me, Maria Eichhorn emphasized the importance of the scrims for the experience of the exhibition, as the translucent light filtering into the space encouraged visitors to linger longer and, as a result, spend more time with the work. Conversation with Maria Eichhorn, August 19, 2021, New York City.

39 The use of the funds was more complex than stated here. In a conversation with John Miller, Eichhorn explains that the 50,000 euros was considered a loan. In addition, documenta GmbH paid for administrative costs related to founding the company, ongoing maintenance, displays, and furniture, and for the publication. The actual stack of 50,000 euros, however, exists. It was considered another material for making the work, "just like wood, paper or any material you use to make an artwork." See Alejandro Cesarco, ed., *Between Artists: Maria Eichhorn, John Miller* (New York: Art Resources Transfer, 2008), 17–18. The Van Abbemuseum repaid the loan to documenta GmbH when it purchased the presentation rights in 2007.

40 Okwui Enwezor served as a supervisory board member. Alexander Alberro points out that Eichhorn's working methodology usually involves having some level of commitment from the commissioning institution, which has taken the form of lectures, renovations to a museum's building, the acquisition of something integral to the project, or, in the case of *Documenta11*, Enwezor's participation on the supervisory board of *Maria Eichhorn Aktiengesellschaft*. See Alexander Alberro, "Specters of Provenance: National Loans, the Königsplatz, and Maria Eichhorn's 'Politics of Restitution,'" *Grey Room* 18 (Winter 2004): 68–69. While embedding an institutional figure into the making or maintenance of the work is important, Eichhorn made it clear, however, that she always retains independence from the institution and avoids at all costs for projects to become institutionalized. Conversation with Maria Eichhorn, August 19, 2021.

41 "Foundation Documents 2002: Articles of Association," in Maria Eichhorn, *Maria Eichhorn Aktiengesellschaft*, 51.

42 In a conversation with John Miller, Eichhorn clarifies questions about share ownership in response to Miller's observation that the company is comprised of shared capital, yet it owns all of its shares. Eichhorn replies: "There are no shareholders—at least most of the time." Miller: "Are there ever times when another entity takes possession of these shares?" Eichhorn: "Yes. I do. Under German law, a company may not continue to hold a substantial portion of its own shares indefinitely." Miller: "So how do you handle this?" Eichhorn: "When the company has held more than ten percent of its own shares, within three years it must transfer them to someone else—in our case, to me. This transfer is effected free of charge. It temporarily transforms the company into an ordinary company with me as an ordinary shareholder. After this, I transfer the shares back to the company." In Cesarco, *Between Artists*, 24–25.

43 The current supervisory board is Tilman Bezzenberger, Charles Esche, and Angelika Nollert.

44 "The company belongs to itself, as it were. That is to say, it ultimately belongs to no one. The company's assets, namely its money, no longer have any relation to the shareholders or to anyone else. The concept of property disappears in this case." See Eichhorn, introduction to *Maria Eichhorn Aktiengesellschaft*, 23.

45 In a conversation with John Miller, Eichhorn states, "The work itself, however, is distinct from the material shown. It is a process or event—not an object in itself. Instead, the activities of people, set in certain time intervals constitute the work." See Cesarco, *Between Artists*, 19.

46 The complete work has been exhibited three times: *Documenta11*, Kassel, Germany (June 8–September 15, 2002); Van Abbemuseum, Eindhoven, The Netherlands (June 2, 2007–November 27, 2009); then extended in the exhibition *Play Van Abbe—Part 1. The Game and the Players*, Van Abbemuseum (November 28, 2009–March 21, 2010); and Kunsthaus Bregenz, Bregenz, Austria (May 10–July 6, 2014). For references and information about this work, see Yilmaz Dziewior, ed., *Maria Eichhorn. Catalogue Raisonné, 1986–2015* (Bregenz: Kunsthaus Bregenz, 2017), 390–399.

47 The ongoing maintenance and administration cause the work to be anything but a static thing, more of a liability, financially, than an asset. Further to this point, see Simon Baier, "Punkt, Pathogenese, Strich," *Texte zur Kunst*, no. 96 (December 2014): 226–230.

48 The components include (1) a call for papers for a workshop on orphaned property in Europe; (2) an open call to the public to conduct research and inform the *Institute* about unlawfully held goods; (3) a presentation in the Neue Galerie of a collection of objects owned by Alexander Fiorino and his family, who lived in Kassel; (4) the presentation in the Neue Galerie of a photo album from the Bundesarchiv, or German Federal Archives; (5) a collection of books exhibited as *Unlawfully Acquired Books from Jewish Ownership*; (6) an actual inventory and assessment of all works of art, antiques, paintings, and other possessions taken from Ahornallee 27 in Breslau 18, owned by David Israel Friedmann; (7) the presentation of auction records from 1935 to 1942 in Berlin, which includes a list of auctioned objects and names of buyers; (8) a library and reading room in Neue Galerie, Kassel; and (9) the website *Rose Valland Institute* (www.rosevallandinstitut.org).

49 The discourse is no doubt initiated and, in many ways, influenced by Eichhorn's own detailed categories outlining what the work does. Organized under the heading "The question of the concept of value," are the subheadings "The concept of value"; "Money, commodity"; "Capital gain by destroying (liquidating) capital"; "Accumulation (increase, growth) of value and the reduction (loss) of value"; "Public nature/accessibility of a work"; "Tradability versus non-tradability, the relations of ownership of a work, copyright"; "Ownership of knowledge"; and "Conditions governing artistic theory and practice and the elimination of such conditions." See Eichhorn, introduction to *Maria Eichhorn Aktiengesellschaft*, 26–27. See also *Maria Eichhorn Aktiengesellschaft*, unpaginated, original 2002 publication produced and distributed during *Documenta11*, which has slight variations in English translations of these headings compared to the later version reproduced for the Van Abbemuseum publication.

50 I am aware that Maria Eichhorn's work comes out of a legacy of conceptual art and is in dialogue with figures such as Seth Siegelaub and many others. Conceptual art has been addressed by numerous critics and art historians, the discourse of which is too abundant to detail within the scope of this book.

51 Carolyn Christov-Bakargiev, "Letter to a Friend," in *dOCUMENTA (13), The Book of Books, Catalog 1/3*, ed. Carolyn Christov-Bakargiev and Chus Martínez (Ostfildern: Hatje Cantz, 2012), 78.

52 Christov-Bakargiev, "Letter to a Friend," 77.

53 With regard to this point as it relates to outside participants, Christov-Bakargiev reminds us, "They contribute to the space of *dOCUMENTA (13)* that aims to explore how different forms of knowledge lie at the heart of the active exercise of reimagining the world. What these participants do, and what they 'exhibit' in *dOCUMENTA (13)*, may or may not be art. However, their acts, gestures, thoughts, and knowledges produce and are produced by circumstances that are readable by art, aspects that art can cope with and absorb. The boundary between what is art and what is not becomes less important." Christov-Bakargiev, "The dance was very frenetic, lively, rattling, clanging, rolling, contorted, and lasted a long time," in *dOCUMENTA (13), The Book of Books, Catalog 1/3*, 31.

54 Simon Sheikh makes valuable observations about the pitfalls of pursuing a curatorial thesis in which exhibition research is undertaken to substantiate an already-predetermined positive position, sacrificing the original concept of a thesis that in fact can be proven false. See Sheikh, "Towards the Exhibition as Research," 32–46.

55 Rogoff, "The Expanded Field," 46.

56 Further to these points, in his essay "The Aesthetics of Singularity" Fredric Jameson observes: "Today therefore we consume, not the work, but the idea of the work.... And the work itself, if we can still call it that, is a mixture of theory and singularity. It is not material—we consume it as an idea rather than a sensory presence—and it is not subject to aesthetic universalism, insofar as each of these artifacts reinvents the very idea of art in a new and non-universalizable form, so that it is in that sense even doubtful whether we should use the general term art at all for such singularity-events." See Fredric Jameson, "The Aesthetics of Singularity," *New Left Review* 101 (March/April 2015): 114.

Section 3: Centre for Contemporary Art Singapore

1 NTU CCA Singapore continues to exist as an institution, although the public-facing components at Gillman Barracks are no longer operational and the number of residencies has been reduced. Ute Meta Bauer remains the director. Karin Oen, the former deputy

director, assumed a new role as principal research fellow in the School of Art, Design, and Media at NTU.

2 NTU CCA Singapore officially opened on October 23, 2013, at Gillman Barracks.

3 The art historian and curator Eugene Tan was at the time Director of Lifestyle at the Singapore Economic Development Board (EDB). He was responsible for initiating the commercial-cultural development at Gillman Barracks, which opened in September 2012, and later spearheading the partnership between NTU and EDB. Tan served as co-curator of the inaugural Singapore Biennale in 2006 and curator of the Singapore Pavilion at the 2005 Venice Biennale. At the time of this writing, he is director of the National Gallery Singapore and the Singapore Art Museum.

4 Sabapathy was a curatorial advisor for the Singapore Art Museum and served as co-chair and curatorial advisor for the Singapore Biennale in 2013 and 2016. He has organized and participated in numerous symposia for the Association of Southeast Asian Nations—Committee on Culture and Information. For a comprehensive overview of his writings, see T. K. Sabapathy, *Writing the Modern: Selected Texts on Art and Art History in Singapore, Malaysia, and Southeast Asia, 1973–2015*, ed. Ahmad Mashadi, Susie Lingham, Peter Schoppert, and Joyce Toh (Singapore: Singapore Art Museum, 2018).

5 Sabapathy's essay "Contemporary Art in Singapore: An Introduction" (1993) provides an account of arts education within the context of the evolution of contemporary art in Singapore. See Sabapathy, "Contemporary Art in Singapore: An Introduction," in *Writing the Modern*, 257–264. Visual arts education was in fact offered in public schools. In 1938, the Nanyang Academy of Fine Arts was founded with a curriculum that, according to Sabapathy, was "not constituted to develop research, but to disseminate prevailing knowledge in order to train school teachers, as officers, and so on. Knowledge was a means for determining certain ends." See T. K. Sabapathy, "The Human Factor," in *Place.Labour.Capital*, ed. Ute Meta Bauer and Anca Rujoiu (Singapore: NTU Centre for Contemporary Art Singapore; Milan: Mousse Publishing, 2018), 14. See also T. K. Sabapathy, *Road to Nowhere: The Quick Rise and Long Fall of Art History in Singapore* (Singapore: Art Gallery at the National Institute of Education, 2010).

6 The leading institutions are the National Gallery of Singapore (opened in 2015); Singapore Art Museum (opened in 1996); the Nanyang Fine Arts Academy, originally founded in 1938, which is projected to merge with LASALLE College of the Arts (founded in 1984) to form the University of the Arts by 2023.

7 Tom Holert, *Knowledge Beside Itself: Contemporary Art's Epistemic Politics* (Berlin: Sternberg Press, 2020), 24–25.

8 The mission stated online on the institution's "About" page as of April 11, 2021: "A national research centre of Nanyang Technolog-

ical University, the NTU Centre for Contemporary Art Singapore focuses on *Spaces of the Curatorial*, addressing the urgencies of our time. A leading international art institution, the Centre is a platform, host and partner creating and driven by dynamic thinking in its three-fold constellation: Residencies Programme, Research and Academic Education and Exhibitions. It brings forth innovative, multi-disciplinary, holistic and experimental forms of emergent artistic and curatorial practices that intersect the present and histories of contemporary art embedded in social, geo-political, geo-cultural spheres with other fields of knowledge." See a revised version of the above on the archive site for "NTU Centre for Contemporary Art Singapore," http://archive.ntu.ccasingapore.org/about/, accessed August 7, 2022. While "place," "labor," and "capital" were the overarching themes for programs and invitations to artist residents between 2013 and 2016, the following three years were programmed under "climates," "habitats," and "environments." These latter topics were considered more explicitly accessible to other science and research interests at the university, potentially helping to forge better collaborations among NTU CCA and the parent institution. Skype conversation with Karin Oen, May 5, 2021. The book *Climates.Habitats.Environments*, edited by Bauer, which archives and expands on the institution's work between 2017 and 2020, was published by MIT Press in 2022.

9 Areas of academic programs in the early years included Museum Studies and Cultural Heritage, Curatorial Practice, Exhibition Design, Public Space, Critical Spatial Practice, and Curating Time-Based Media.

10 Ute Meta Bauer, "The Making of an Institution," in *Place.Labour.Capital*, 34–35.

11 The process of selecting artists-in-residence is quite complex. The team solicits nominations from a global network of curators, artists, and writers. The nominated artists are invited to apply, stating why the residency will benefit their work and how their work will contribute to the overarching theme explored by NTU CCA at the time. The proposal is reviewed by a committee composed of Bauer, her team, and members of arts organizations in the region and elsewhere. Skype conversation with Karin Oen, May 5, 2021; email exchange with Anna Lovecchio, October 15, 2021.

12 In 2016, Bauer served as guest editor of a book in the *Jahresring* series, one of the longest-running annual publication series in Germany dedicated to contemporary art and literature. Her edition, *SouthEastAsia: Spaces of the Curatorial*, focuses a wide lens on the expansive approaches to curating in Southeast Asia. Part of the point of the volume is to map the wide-ranging curatorial initiatives, artist-run spaces, and collectives that compose the interconnected regional arts scene, robust and thriving despite the challenges of public funding and the psychological and physical traces of colonialism. See Ute Meta Bauer and Brigette Oetker,

eds., *SouthEastAsia: Spaces of the Curatorial*, Jahresring 63 (Singapore: NTU Centre for Contemporary Art Singapore; Berlin: Sternberg Press, 2016).

13 Between her time at OCA Norway, where she founded the journal *Verksted*, and her appointment as founding director of NTU CCA in 2013, Bauer was director of MIT's Visual Arts Program from 2005 to 2009; there she reimagined the graduate curriculum in visual arts to launch MIT's program in Art, Culture, and Technology, for which she served as director from 2009 to 2012. Earlier, she had served as professor of Theory and Practice of Contemporary Art at the Academy of Fine Arts Vienna from 1996 to 2006. From 1990 to 1994, she was director of Künstlerhaus Stuttgart where she founded the annual magazine titled *Meta*.

14 Bauer was the first to address in print the intersections of public and private interests in the arts during the early years of her directorship at OCA Norway. See Bauer, foreword to "New Institutionalism," ed. Jonas Ekeberg, *Verksted* 1 (2003): 5–7. This is a subject about which I've previously written; see James Voorhies, *Beyond Objecthood: The Exhibition as a Critical Form since 1968* (Cambridge, MA: MIT Press, 2017).

15 *The Making of an Institution* comprised four sections with titles appropriated from the form of a public report, the type of report required by governing bodies that administer and provide support to institutions like NTU CCA. The sections were titled *Reason to Exist: The Director's Review*; *Ownership, Development, and Aspirations*; *Artistic Research*; and *Communication and Mediation*. One of the more salient takeaways from the sweeping "report" was that NTU CCA was moving too fast and not taking into account other constituents. Bauer and her team learned that they could slow the pace of exhibitions, involve other organizations and university departments in programs, share resources, and communicate more broadly to regional stakeholders in order to build stronger audiences while fulfilling wider national agendas that may not have been on the immediate radar, like fostering cultural development and supporting knowledge economies. Skype conversation with Ute Meta Bauer, April 29, 2021.

16 Membership gave visitors access to read the books in the library. Members were not permitted to borrow books. On the first page of each book in the library is the statement: "This book is a part of 'The Library of Unread Books,' an artist-run space initiated by Heman Chong in 2016. The library is made up of books from the shelves of individuals which are unread by their previous owners." Heman Chong, "The Book of Drafts (Part 2)," in *Place.Labour. Capital*, 77.

17 This has become more apparent as the number of titles and variety of subjects in the library has grown to over two thousand titles since its debut in Singapore in 2017; since then, it has traveled to venues in Manila, Utrecht, Milan, Dubai, the Czech Republic, and back to Singapore in 2020.

18 Chong's text "The Book of Drafts (Part 2)" and a reproduction of his painting *A History of Amnesia* (2016) are reproduced in *Place. Labour.Capital*, 76–81.

19 They included Diana Campbell Betancourt, artistic director of Samdani Art Foundation and chief curator of Dhaka Art Summit, in Dhaka, Bangladesh; Maria Hlavajova from BAK in Utrecht, the Netherlands; Sanne Oorthuizen and Alec Steadman, co-chief curators at Cemeti at the Institute for Art and Society, Yogyakarta, Indonesia; Emily Pethick from the Showroom in London; and Farah Wardani, assistant director of the Resource Centre at the National Gallery Singapore.

20 Participants included åbäke, Bahbak Hashemi-Nezhad, Wilfried Kuehn, Christoph Knoth, Bastian von Lehsten, and Laura Miotto.

21 From her years as director of Künstlerhaus in Stuttgart (1990–1994), Bauer has consistently looked to publications as a valuable form of public address. *Meta*, the annual magazine she launched while at Künstlerhaus, was published for four years and became an essential outlet for communicating about programming at Künstlerhaus while also serving as a way to extend the physical exhibition into printed matter. Maria Lind's interview of Bauer for the book *Künstlerhaus Stuttgart. 40 Jahre 1978–2018* offers an insightful view into Bauer's work. Bauer talks about *Meta*, her commitment to publications, and her early experiments with what would eventually be referred to as the curatorial. See Hannelore Paflik-Huber, ed., *Künstlerhaus Stuttgart. 40 Jahre 1978–2018* (Stuttgart: Künstlerhaus Stuttgart, 2020).

22 Sabapathy, "The Human Factor," 17.

23 Chus Martínez, "How a Tadpole Becomes a Frog: Belated Aesthetics, Politics, and Animated Matter. Toward a Theory of Artistic Research," in *dOCUMENTA (13), The Book of Books, Catalog 1/3*, ed. Carolyn Christov-Bakargiev and Chus Martínez (Ostfildern: Hatje Cantz, 2012), 47–48.

Exact Imagination

1 My understanding and interpretation of Adorno's "exact imagination" is indebted to Shierry Weber Nicholsen's magisterial book *Exact Imagination, Late Work: On Adorno's Aesthetics* (Cambridge, MA: MIT Press, 1997). Nicholsen points out that Adorno referred to the concept of "exact imagination" [*exakte Phantasie*] throughout much of his writing. Two notable appearances are in his 1931 lecture "The Actuality of Philosophy" and a 1965 radio talk called "Schöne Stellen" (Beautiful passages). For English translations, see "The Actuality of Philosophy" (1931), *Telos* 31 (spring 1977): 120–133, and an excerpt of the radio program is reprinted as "Little Heresy" (1965), in Richard Leppert, ed., Susan H. Gillespie, trans., *Theodor W. Adorno: Essays on Music* (Berkeley: University of California, 2002), 318–324. Analyzing music

comprehension, Adorno writes, "The whole and the parts cannot be so fully merged into each other as an aesthetic ideal that is by no means limited to classicism demands. The right way to hear music includes a spontaneous awareness of the non-identity of the whole and the parts as well as of the synthesis that unites the two." Whereas, for Adorno, "It makes sense that the way to understand the whole would have to lead up from the individual part, as well as down from the whole. Musical experience is all the more impelled to take this route since there are no longer any overarching forms to which the ear could entrust itself blindly. The means to such experience is exact imagination (*exakte Phantasie*). It opens up the richness of the individual detail, over which it lingers, instead of hastening past it to the whole." Adorno, "Little Heresy," 321–322. I'm grateful to Nicholsen for pointing my attention to these published translations, amid the vast corpus of Adorno's writing. Email exchange with Shierry Weber Nicholsen, July 26, 2021.

2 In the context of theorizing philosophy as something nondiscursive, or not fully beholden to language, Adorno writes, "An exact imagination; an imagination that remains strictly confined to the material offered it by scholarship and science and goes beyond them only in the smallest features of its arrangement, features which of course it must produce of itself." Here, I've cited Nicholson's translation in her book, where she translates "exakte Phantasie" as "exact imagination" rather than "precise fantasy." It's believed Adorno intended to evoke Kant and the aesthetic rather than Freud. See Nicholsen, *Exact Imagination*, 4, n.9, 229.

3 According to Nicholsen, "Adorno formulates the essential feature of late work as the disjunction of subjectivity and objectivity, so that as work becomes late it becomes increasingly inorganic. In this sense, late work characterizes the direction the arts take as modernism advances within the context of 'late capitalism,' a phrase Adorno, too, uses." Nicholsen, *Exact Imagination*, 8.

4 Quoted in Nicholsen, *Exact Imagination*, 35.

5 T. J. Demos, "Curating against the Apocalypse, *Documenta 13*, 2012," in *Curating and Politics beyond the Curator: Initial Reflections*, ed. Heidi Bale Amundsen and Gerd Elise (Ostfildern: Hatje Cantz, 2015), 80.

6 Tom Holert, "Being Concerned? Scattered Thoughts on 'Artistic Research' and 'Social Responsibility,'" in *Intellectual Birdhouse: Artistic Practice as Research*, ed. Ute Meta Bauer, Florian Dombois, Claudia Mareis, and Michael Schwab (London: Koenig Books, 2012), 27–28.

7 I am indebted here and elsewhere to Irit Rogoff's astute interpretation and analysis of the relationship between knowledge and curating, and how both inform the curatorial. Her October 2013 lecture in Hong Kong, in particular, is illuminating. See "Irit Rogoff: The Exhibition as an Event of Knowledge Production," lecture, Asia Art Archive, October 2013, https://aaa.org.hk/en/programmes/programmes/irit-rogoff-the-exhibition-as-an-event-of-knowledge-production, accessed August 7, 2022.

8 "Irit Rogoff: The Exhibition as an Event of Knowledge Production."

9 Irit Rogoff, "Becoming Research," in *What Museums Do: The Curatorial in Parallax*, ed. Choi Jina and Helen Jungyeon Ku (Seoul: National Museum of Modern and Contemporary Art, 2018), 45–46.